THOUGHT FOR FOOD

Thought For Food is the first print book published by South Broadway Press. Proceeds raised from the sales of this book will go to support Denver Food Rescue. Learn more about Denver Food Rescue at www.denverfoodrescue.org.

We respectfully acknowledge that this book was created on the traditional, ancestral, unceded territory of the Cheyenne, Arapaho and Ute People who have stewarded this land throughout generations. With this same respect, we acknowledge this book was printed on the land of the Catawba People.

THOUGHT FOR FOOD

An Anthology of Poems Benefiting Denver Food Rescue

South Broadway Press | Denver CO

SOUTH BROADWAY PRESS

Published by South Broadway Press
South Broadway Press LLC, 1152 Fillmore St Denver CO 80206, USA

First published in the United States of America by South Broadway Press, 2020

Copyright © South Broadway Press, 2020
All rights reserved

Poems in this anthology have appeared previously in the following places:

Cover Image: Lewis Neeff

THE LIBRARY OF CONGRESS HAS CATALOGED THE PAPERBACK
EDITION AS FOLLOWS:
2020941255 Press, South Broadway
Thought For Food: An Anthology of Poems Benefiting Denver Food Rescue

ISBN (pbk.) 978-1-7350355-0-5

Printed in the United States of America

Edited by Emylee Frank, Kali Heals, Erica Hoffmeister and Brice Maiurro

Except in the United States of America, this book is sold subject to the condition that it shall not, by way of trade or otherwise, be lent, re-sold, hired out, or otherwise circulated without the publisher's prior consent in any form of binding or cover other than that which it is published and without a similar condition including this condition being imposed on the subsequent purchaser.

The scanning, uploading and distribution of this book via the Internet or via any other means without the permission of the publisher is illegal and punishable by law. Please purchase online authorized electronic editions, and do not participate in or encourage electronic piracy of copyrighted materials. Your support of the authors' rights is appreciated.

www.soboghoso.org

www.denverfoodrescue.org

THOUGHT FOR FOOD

An Anthology of Poems Benefiting Denver Food Rescue

Edited by
Emylee Frank, Kali Heals,
Erica Hoffmeister & Brice Maiurro

NOTES FROM THE EDITORS

EMYLEE FRANK

In a period of uncertainty, little moments of tranquility and distance from the chaos around you are crucial. While watching COVID-19 sweep the globe, it became increasingly hard to find those moments for myself. The impact that this pandemic will have on our human collective isn't fathomable as I am writing this. Through contributing and editing Thought For Food, I finally found myself with time where I could sit with myself and reflect on the happenings around us. As I read through each expression, each voice, I felt so immersed with emotion, and reassured by a sense of community. In a chapter of history that has felt so lonely, it was almost spiritual to realize that we were all united in this. With every piece of art created during COVID-19 we can create a moment of tranquility and hopefully give that gift to one another. I hope as you journey through these pages -- these individual experiences, expressions, stories, thoughts, and lives -- you are able to breathe in that happiness and embrace the connection we all hold.

ERICA HOFFMEISTER

One thing has been made clear through the COVID-19 pandemic crisis, and that is the natural human inclination for community spaces. After several weeks of feeling overwhelmed and having a difficult time creatively in isolation, my empath sensors triggered by the world's events witnessing communities crumble and struggle, I was unsurprised by who stepped up to provide community care and mutual aid in response: the creatives. I am so indelibly proud and grateful to have the opportunity to gather (virtually) with the amazing Denver writing community and team at South Broadway Press to *act* and not only create and distribute art (which is, on its own a form of emotional care and aid) but also monetary, tangible help with the production of this anthology. The quality of work we have read, and the support we've been met with through this process has been an experience of joy and healing, and I am so happy to share our labor of love and community with everyone. A very sincere thank you to contributors, donors, and readers—we are truly all connected by experience, love, and the poetry in everything.

KALI HEALS

In a time of isolation, one may feel required to stay inside by law or health concerns. Of course, some stay in their home. But some decide to go deeper; into the depth of their consciousness; into the ideas they hold dear; into the interior of their soul. You may choose, when your gut says "Do something!", to distract yourself or to examine and reexamine your convictions and how you are upholding those. This, I think, is the difficult gift of our strange quarantime. I would like to thank our poets, supporters and contributors for doing just that. The writings herein have touched my heart, mind & spirit, as I hope they do for our readers. My wish for those who are experiencing alone time in a new way is that when you find boredom, frustration, loneliness… that you are able to sit with it. And also let it be a gateway. May tough times be times when you reach in for deeper mastery of yourself, when you reach out and find greater closeness with your friends, and when you are called in and out to experience ever deeper understanding and appreciation of your community and your soul. I have so much gratitude to you all for your vulnerability & kindness. It makes me honored to be involved in community outreach and editing for South Broadway Press & Ghost Society. Thank you all. Truly.

BRICE MAIURRO

It's been a really beautiful experience witnessing the alchemy of all these poems, moments and stories come together into one collection. In these times of COVID and social isolation, it is astounding how interconnected we are in what we are feeling. Our experiences are all different, yes, but nonetheless connected. These poems are filled with the love of food and community, with the anxiety of separation. They are filled with a melancholic reflection on where we've been fused with this quiet hope of where we are headed, especially in relationship to this planet and as a part of nature. The poems are raw and brutal and sometimes very endearing and kind, especially as a reminder to be kind to one another as we all endure this hardship together. I am just so happy to have the chance to read these poems and put them together in a collection. Thank you to all of you who took the time in so many ways to make this collection a reality.

TABLE OF CONTENTS

Ars Poetica: Access | Cortney Collins 1
Pomegranate Blues | Brett Randell 3
The Alley Poets | Chelsea Cook 4
open hand | Patricia McCrystal 6
Things you don't say at the dinner… | Bruce Sterling 7
My Mother's Recipe | Jovan Mays, Mallary McHenry Jr. 8
How the Sunflower Practices… | Maria S. Picone 13
Bacon | Caleb Ferganchick 14
Alphabet Soup | Nate Ragolia 17
The Mechanics of Food Assistance…| Dennis Etzel Jr. 18
#5 April 2020 | Ted Vaca 19
Love in the Time of Covid | Stina French 21
Untitled Haiku | Iris Groot 23
FOR THE WANT OF YOU | Liza Sparks 24
Tomato Red | Sophie Cardin 25
I Will Wait for You, Little Strawberry | Shelsea Ochoa 27
Fuck Yes! Soufflé | Kevin Quinn Marchman 29
HOWL | Charles Dalton Telschow 31
Bread in the air | Ashley Howell Bunn 33
Eve | Amy Wray Irish 34
Ripe Apples | Jessica Rigney 35
Hunger | Christopher Woods 37
A Winter's Night | Varinia Rodriguez 38
YUM | Caito Foster 40
None of That | Anna Leahy 42

Pretzels	Danny Mazur	44
The Sound of One Howl…	Roseanna Frechette	46
I feared I was a werewolf	Jericho Hockett	47
The Motherfuckin' Broccoli	Irina Bogomolova	48
On My Mother's Birthday…	David Zaworski	52
Say a Mass for Me Today	Daniel G. Snethen	53
Postal Distancing	Steve Shultz	55
Believing in a Troubled God	Bill Gainer	58
Hunger is an Excellent Cook	Brendan Hamilton	59
Untitled	Sarah LaRue	61
License Plates on the Barn Wall	Guinotte Wise	62
Yeggman Blues	Catfish McDaris	64
Pandemic Escapees	Leah Mueller	65
Nothing is the Other's Blinding	Liam Max Kelley	67
Thou Shalt Not Lock the Fucking Door	Matt Clifford	69
This is not the cool dystopia…	Lonnie MF Allen	71
Toilet Paper Blues	Jane Ripley	74
Virtual Easter	Jennifer Faylor	76
Drunk at King…	Jonathan Bluebird Montgomery	77
Dick Dale Cures the 'Rona	Shawn Pavey	81
How to Slice Open…	Rosemerry Wahtola Trommer	83
On the Trail	Michael Sage	84
SEA	Umar Nizar	86
is I'm not	Jake Riley	87
it will not matter	Scout Noa Halpern	89
Speak to Me	Emylee Frank	91
OCCUPY LOVE	Judyth Hill	94
Los saguaros are being destroyed	Marcy Rae Henry	95
What a Gift to be Born into Darkness	Kali Heals	97
Let It Be	Arlis Mongold	99
remembrance	Sarah Jane Justice	100

This is a Test | Eli Whittington	101
Three Blue Apron Found Poems | s. Nicholas	103
To Melons | Gerard Sarnat	106
For the Sad Waitress at… | Alexis Rhone Fancher	108
Belief | Taylor Jones	110
Pepper | Jeff Burt	112
the problem with talking love | Rebecca Hannigan	113
About My Breasts, Since You Asked | Sherre Vernon	116
Gutting the Deer | Cicada Musselman	121
Twenty Seconds or Death | Rob Geisen	122
Love Poem from an Avocado | Lee Frankel Goldwater	127
Quarantine Dinner | Liza Katz Duncan	128
The Four-Year Itch | Hannah Skewes	130
Quotidian Delivery | Kierstin Bridger	132
In Other News | Eric Raanan Fischman	134
Ode to the Avocado | Tricia Knoll	135
All Am I, I Am All | Robert Beveridge	137
Roses Encased in Glass… | Gwendalynn Roebke	138
I am the invasive knotweed | Caroline Savery	139
Isolation is My Destiny | Syed Aamir Sharief Qadri	141
DYING FREE | mayryanna	143
Tomatoes | Mary Christine Delea	145
Live is a Strange Word | Grace Mitchell	147
Your Handwriting | Steven Sassman	148
A.T. | John Staughton	150
Scream | Veronica Love	154
You are not meditating | Agnes Vojta	156
Good vs. Typical | Connor Orrico	158
Blue Boy | Kristin LaFollette	159
Mother's Day Conversations… | Nicole Taylor	161

Jeff Bezos | Brice Maiurro 164
Signed up for a 365 Day… | Maggie Saunders 166
There's a Particular Way… | Erica Hoffmeister 167
Hock Messer | Wendy Mannis Scher 170
Día de los Muertos | Ken Farrell 171
The Invisible Indispensable | Galen Bernard 173
Moussaka | Janette Schafer 175
Hunger Map | Anna White 176
The Best Way to Eat a Grape | Deborah Edler Brown 178

The Kitchen is the Soul… | Morgan L. Ventura 179
Some Afternoon | Riley Welch 182
Christmas Cookies | David-Matthew Barnes 183
Two Poems | Mary Anna Kruch 184
4:36 am | Jacob Ian DeCoursey 189
A Pandemic Note to Self | Hayden Dansky 190
The Return | Melissa Ferrer 195
Traditio, Patron Saint of Legacy | Paulie Lipman 199

THOUGHT FOR FOOD

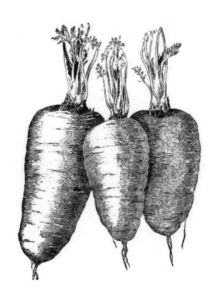

Ars Poetica: Access | Cortney Collins

An award-winning photojournalist once told me

anyone can learn to take a good photo.

It's not technique.

It's access.

Access:

to a riot breaking out on an angry street.

to a woman who has just lost her finger
climbing over a chain-link fence
crossing the border into Texas.

to the dusty rubble,
and everything beneath,
moments after a bomb
has incinerated a home.

to a sun-washed bedroom
where a seven year old child
has just died of cancer
in his mother & father's arms.

Poetry is not just metaphor and meter,
allegory and alliteration.

Poetry is access:

to the secret hobbies of protozoans.

to the color of chlorophyll.

to the lover you secretly yearn for
but know will destroy you.

to enough magic to bring
your cat back from a velvet
bag of ashes embroidered
with his name.

A poem can only be

what it can access.

Pomegranate Blues | Brett Randell

grape grape
apple apple
pomegranate blues
smokin' in the alleyway
moonlit dancin' shoes

mint mint
lemon lemon
garlic ginger waltz
old man in the dining hall
says it's not his fault

citrus citrus
honey honey
echinacea poem
cursed if you go out to play
blessed if you stay home

lime lime
dandelion
stingin' nettle song
bright eyed baby lookin' up
wonderin' what went wrong

The Alley Poets | Chelsea Cook

Let me show you
Where the poets live.
They gather in an alley, at midnight, under the full moon,
To read dirty haiku and make a ruckus in the streets.

Rebels!
But they are caring rebels.

Tonight, I found the alley poets
And took a dose of love.
How are you feeling? they ask.
Good, I say.
(Good is always the right answer, the work answer.)
No, tell us how you really feel.
Depressed.
That's better, because it's honest. Now come here:
"Every day, we'll show you a moment so golden you must close your eyes to see it."
I must stick around for that day.

Why is death such a theme in poetry?
Why does the depressed mind latch onto it,
Instead of the beauty in the words, the rhymes, the repetition?
Why is it so easy for pain to enter,
For negative feelings to take root like weeds,
For the analytical mind to try and rationalize the irrational?

The alley poets tell me a ghost story:
About the monster "that which follows"!

Stalking the cities, the towns, the towers
For those souls whose hearts have turned to stone.
It is insatiable, all-consuming, leaving destruction in its wake.
But they also tell me:
"That which follows" hates fire, warmth, light, love.

So, the alley poets light a campfire.
We sing and dance and read,
Keeping the darkness at bay.
Not to sound cliché
But the poems they recite,
Are the stars between the clouds at night.

They hug me tightly as I take my leave,
Encouraging: I must carry the ember until the next time
The community comes together.
The upbeat music starts to play,
Because…"that which follows" has no chance
Against the alley poets!

open hand | Patricia McCrystal

morning croaked open: mountain bluebirds, mourning
doves, white-throated swifts, freshwater voice pulls me
salted and bruised from hard dreams lightninged through,
veined with parted heart-swallows, ropey future what-ifs

your morning skin on inhale a nod to my toddler god:
carnal recall of lived-in cotton, baby blanket I clutched to
my face, shredded vessel of unconditioned hard-rubbed
love—

how is it you bring this gift? I forgot what forged me. You
reek of origin. A stone, there, see me
wedged in earth, pushing my weight forth, rippling your
heart around my jagged thrust,
your mouth, wet surface, new womb

born an open hand, I discovered safety in fist. Each grief a
finger folded. No
was my home

I unfold this bundle of sharp joints & bury them in your
riverbed, press down with open hands
will I be drowned? will I be
rounded from ragged stone

morning swims to me faithful as sunrise: mountain
bluebirds, mourning doves, warm-tided
song in your throat
cadence: warn cotton of remember
crescendo: you, my soft loop of future

Things you don't say at the dinner table, which in my case growing up was anything. | Bruce Sterling

I avoided speaking for fear of communication
or maybe humiliation.
I didn't know how to talk
or specifically
to speak their language without reprisal.

Slipping up in our household was tantamount to losing
and losing was bad
and bad is how I felt
for much of my life.
See shame runs deep
in my family
which
coincidentally is quite a shame.

My Mother's Recipe |
Jovan Mays and Mallary McHenry Jr.

When we were young
we didn't appreciate our mother's cooking.
We would stare at the plate
willing broccoli to GO AWAY.
But today is different.

I remember hearing Cindy Lawrie
ask for the recipe of her favorite dish
& my mother explained
that she could not duplicate this.
This was my mother's bread of sorrows.

I remember it.
She said,
"when makin' sweet bread
we need a bowl the size of Birmingham.
Make sure it's not segregated
I want everyone to feast."

She would say,
"My butter was churned by hand.
Milked from my motherland.
Takin' the same milk of my history,
diluting my people to livestock,
skimming off the backs of blacks
to build Antebellum houses
that made the South
want to rise again like cornbread."

She wasn't just a cook in that kitchen.

Full time doctor-alchemist-magician.
She could make that cream
cook, cleanse, & cure.

When friends asked her about margarine,
She laughed, said
"Margarine is made of pretty things"
40 acres & a mule,
equality, reparations,
straight hair, & freedom.
Things that just were not real.

So no!
She did not use margarine
She used butter
thick, unrelenting,
get-all-over-everything butter.
the kind you have to strain to bind.

Like sitting in the back of balconies & buses.
"Churn it"
Like having dry ice thrown at her
because she was a different type of sugar.
"Churn it more"

Sometimes she would have to take over for me.
Because I didn't understand that she was erasing the past
with
Every.   Single.   Agitation.
Wondering why she would tear up.
"You have to churn it, boy!"

'Till the south is too suppressed to rise.

'Till it's white & entitled
like Bull Connor's tank in an all-black neighborhood.
Like them shepherds k9's sinking into our skin.

"Beat it!
So they can't see the darkness in this meal.
Beat it!
Like a white hood just appeared in this room.
Let me show you how painful this is."

& she refuses to forget,
because going through restaurant drive-thru windows
still feels like you're going around the back.

& you wonder why you need water to wash this down.
Because if you didn't, you would feel the countless
Butter-worth Jemimas climbing your esophagus
with wooden spoons & spatulas.

Wash it down
until your gut feels like a hull.
Bet you didn't know that in the belly of your ship
there were grunts paddling your digestion
no wonder it's called the Middle Passage.

To this day I wonder what kept her
cooking for friends like Cindy Lawrie.
What kept her from back handing them every time
they asked her "Alfreda what did you put in this?"
or "Mrs. McHenry" can I get that recipe?"

She would always say,
"Give thanks to God for all things"
The good & the bad.
Martin Luther King Jr. & James Earl Ray.
John Brown & Jim Crow.
Shining steeples & burnt crosses.

THIS
makes her flour.
It's forgiveness.
Forgiveness isn't big on measuring.
Forgiveness isn't big on accuracy.
Just like my momma.

A pinch of salt here.
Like her father waiting
at Sears and Roebucks until
closing before whites would
let him buy clothes.

A sprinkle of sugar there.
Her remembering the day
she was allowed to enter a library
alongside white people.

In the spirit of Nat Turner, Emmet Till, 4 little girls.
Momma is whisking together gender & race.
Hopes & dreams.
The past to the present.

& the secret, she told us was,
"Son, just keep tasting
'till you get the flavor you want.

Until, there are no more tears.
Just keep tasting
until the anger becomes harmonious.
Just keep tasting
until the sadness becomes savory.
Just. Keep. Tasting."

But this isn't store bought processed white bread.
THIS IS MY MOTHER'S BREAD OF SORROWS
& now Cindy Lawrie you can have this recipe.
But you still can't make this dish

How the Sunflower Practices a Distancing | Maria S. Picone

Fortifying her core, she sips a poverty of water,
muting the fresh-corn brilliance of her body
with white curtains. She awaits a joy bobbin
to hover at her concentric breast. She knows
a scarred Saturday implies renewal.
Instincts tell her: *wait, respire, listen.*
Turning her face skyward, she takes
her mother's gifts: rain, the hum of bees.

Bacon | Caleb Ferganchick

It is 6AM on a Monday
and I am standing in the kitchen preparing breakfast.
On any other Monday I would have recognized this obscurity
as the manic episode it is, pop a hydroxyzine
to ease the crushing anxiety of false optimism
washing over me like the covers I'd pull back
over my body until the doctor could see me again.
I've learned my emotions are like Mondays,
tidal waves that roll over me with a force I cannot control,
and I don't know if its these smoker's lungs
or a lifetime of coping mechanisms that never keep me afloat,
but swimming is an exercise
that has always resulted in drowning.

But on this particular Monday,
Love slinks out of the bedroom.

Love slinks out of the bedroom with the audacity to be perfect,
with tousled hair and sleep clinging to his eyes
that makes me fear perhaps I grasped too tightly in the night,
clasped on to his body like a buoy in the harbor
former sailors have mistaken for their sanctuary,
intending to restore their masts on the days when sunshine implores me
to be the band-aid on the world's sails, only to hoist them up

in the gale of my storm ridden seas in search of calmer
waters.

I am worried that if I share these things with Love
my words will flash like beams of light permeating
from some rocky outpost, imploring him to heed the warning
of ships drowned by waves that rose with no warning.

But Love's smile breaks the shivering dawn
and he plants a weary kiss on my lips as if to say,
"Let's be castaways together."

I think that maybe, on this particular Monday,
it's very possible Love and mania are the same.
I think that maybe, instead of medicating Love,
I want to cook him breakfast.

I think so what if I rarely have the resolve
to care for my own body, so what
if my queer is not culinary inclined?

I remember how it struck me suddenly
that he was a sunflower suspended
on an endless seascape horizon,
and what is a poet's lot in life
save to nurture flowers?

Somewhere between the rich soil of black coffee beans
and the scramble of whipping eggs
I manage to burn the bacon.

The lighthouse is now a smoke alarm.

The ocean an iron skillet.

Monday is a Monday.

It is 6AM.

But Love,
Love eats the bacon anyway.

Alphabet Soup | Nate Ragolia

Buried corn spilt milk
What good is a food system
when it doesn't feed?

Can you believe it? We're actually throwing away tens of millions of pounds of fresh vegetables, fruits? We're doing it because "it can't be moved" and "nothing is *EVER* free." But couldn't we make some Alphabet Soup? Job the jobless, move the food, set a new goal that if we have so much that we'd trash it we'd be smarter and kinder and truer to Greatness by finding every open mouth and grumbling gut and filling them with sustenance—if rarely meaning, here—because there'd be at least one bold checkmark in the WIN column? Think of the Ratings! MILLIONS RE-EMPLOYED TO DO SOMETHING PURPOSEFUL, MILLIONS MORE *NOT* STARVING IN THE CORNERS AND NOOKS OF OUR PREPOSTEROUS OPULENCE.

Oh, The Supply Chain!
Chickens dead, landfills filling
Waste not? *Want!* Always.

The Mechanics of Food Assistance in a Grocery Store Line | Dennis Etzel Jr.

what is taking so long? someone asks
with plastic card in hand
I will still hand over supplemental checks
like nails that board up a boat

I call them life savers out of needa
even for these staples
while a scan and rescan of each item
ensures eligibility because even if WIC stickers

are misplaced on the shelves the register
has the final say and I am ready so ready
to turn around if someone gives me the drill
or again remarks *it must be nice to get free food*

I'll iron out their words with my defenses
hey I'm a working professor and father
adding how I qualify as poor how my wife and I
were drilled at the food assistance office

hammered by every question
from someone who speaks in the tone
of a kindergarten teacher so my boys
will have food at the end of the month

unlike so many children in this town
even the retired chaplain who overheard
kids could get a free lunch
said *why don't they get a job?*

*Previously appeared in Bards Against Hunger: Kansas

#5 April 2020 | Ted Vaca

for those that feel

for the mind can not
       touch

you

me

we hold each other so close
we squeeze
merge

break through the distance
back from the moon
circle around the globe

I sit next to you
you ask me if the canyon spirit
is going to die

we shelter in place
on a small bench
by the fountain
in Civic Center
surrounded by trees

"we have to rely
on ourselves
to keep it alive"
I say

the wind blows
people are howling
and their loneliness
and yearning
for all that they once held
burns through the dusk

you ask me if
I can feel it

"feel what" I ask

"the wild return"
you say

"of what"
I say

"of everything we ever loved
 and never could tame"

Love in the Time of Covid | Stina French

Before you got laid off, you worked for Enterprise,
with no sick leave and no wage protection.

You said even the car rentals in Italy were open.
Your roommate feared you'd infect her.
You were the only one who had to leave for work.
You were the only person of color in your house.

You aren't afraid to die, but, older than you, I am.
In Milan, lines of hearses haul coffins to cremation.
Their drivers can't stay home, either:
hospitals have no more room to burn bodies.

During a virtual appointment one week into quarantine,
my doctor says a newly diagnosed thyroid disease
puts me in the at-risk group.
She says, don't become inflamed.

I am putting out fires inside other fires,
but you keep your cool.
You're out there somewhere,
listening to sunrise.
It feels like I had to shut the door
before you got inside.

We don't know how long it will be this way.
Sometimes we walk the dog, 6-feet apart,
not holding hands or hugging.
We sleep real late;
we howl at eight;
we send video of ourselves cumming.

I make careful grocery lists,
ask for rice, oatmeal, sweet potatoes.
You deliver.

I don't touch anything you bring
until it's wiped or sits three days,
but this morning,
my mouth knew your love
as a mango it didn't ask for.

Untitled Haiku | Iris Groot

I wish I could say
I left you behind when I
drove across country

FOR THE WANT OF YOU | Liza Sparks

I am shaking for the want of you
I am sweating for the want of you
I am biting my bottom lip

I am casting spells for the want of you
I am planting seeds for the want of you
I am drinking love potions

I am sewing & mending for the want of you
I am writing heart songs for the want of you
I am kissing trees

I am dancing in meadows for the want of you
I am spinning silly for the want of you
I am howling at the moon

I am eating honey & dates so you'll be sweet for me
I am lighting candles so you'll burn for me
I am writing your name over & over again
I am sipping spirits to intoxicate you with me
I am tying strings together to connect you with me
I am tracing your name on my skin

I am chanting your name into my garden
I am whispering your name into the wind
I am drumming your name into the mountain
I am throwing coins into wells
I am making wishes on stars
I am praying to any amulet, any symbol, any god that will listen
                                      all for the want of you

Tomato Red | Sophie Cardin

give it to me tomato red
spread out like
flour all over the counter
cold on my back

mouths burning with
salsa and impulse

cover me with thyme
and brown sugar

dip your fingertips
in the spice jars and let me guess
what is what and which is which

I am gasping, caffeinated, like
the flame marked moka pot,
older than you, than I,
than us both together,
older than this dance, older

than the mothers, and their
pleasure, and their kitchens
filled with smells

leave me someplace warm
so I can rise, in the sun

want feasts on the body
like yeast, souring
as it chews through wheat

the basil is growing from seed
alongside salvaged potato eyes
which watch our backs

I cover everything in cilantro
but you soap-tongued screw
up your face at the taste of it
so I smear honey on my lips, and
bid you lick it off

I sink my hands, up to the elbow
into containers of rice and beans
fancying rain that won't come till summer

cool like dried legumes and
fine like grains

I draw pictures
in the coffee grounds
spilt at breakfast

run hot water over my hands
until they are red and pink knuckled
wet and clean

I Will Wait for You, Little Strawberry | Shelsea Ochoa

I will wait for you,
Little strawberry

I knew you when you were just a little flower
With your yellow belly to the sun
I watched you dancing in the wind
Beaming, being, feeding bees
Held by a beautiful mother plant
Her deep roots locked into the wet soil like a complicated code
Her sturdy leafs collecting light for your existence
You have always been almost pure existence

Now, you are a little green bloop of a thing
I love how you hold your seeds on the outside,
Making it very clear to the birds that may eat you
That being delicious comes second
To a purpose beyond a single strawberry

In this crazy world of squirrels and crows
Nothing in life is guaranteed
So I will not wait to enjoy you
Now, as you are
Hard and green and in-between
I enjoy the wait

Just as I enjoyed the idea of you when you were nothing but an idea
I will enjoy the memory of you once only memory remains
And *squeee* maybe one day I will get to take a juicy bite

Of something so sweet and sunkissed and ruby and
dazzling and bold and wow and life and pop and slurp
and drippy and mmm!

I will wait for you, little strawberry
Just in case I get the chance

Fuck Yes! Soufflé | Kevin Quinn Marchman

1. One big ole frying pan. Not just big, but special. You need to decide what shape you want this to come out as. Maybe a stage, or easel or maybe a you-shaped frying pan, but it has gotta be big.

2. Add one cup of vision. Imagine this delicious, gleaming, steaming hot soufflé as the centerpiece.

3. Like, 73 parts preparation. Have each bite, individual flavor and texture of this tasty ass creation mapped out. This ain't just food, its architecture! Mise-en-place!

4. Vigorously mix that with a dose of expectation and realization. It ain't gonna look, taste, smell, feel like the picturesque shit you just envisioned. It's gonna be great, but unexpected. Maybe even better than the meal you had the capacity to imagine at the start of this process.

5. Now you gotta cook. You need a lot of heat. And regular ass fire ain't gonna cut. No electric, butane, propane or charcoal is gonna cut it. You need some powerful kindling to feed this flame. Pressure, passion, fear, desire, divine inspiration, bullshit, clarity, fun, more fun, frustration, drugs, and love. So much love. Alla dat.

Tip: Cooking time is trickier. You can cook for 1 second or 30 years and still can't be sure it's made to satisfaction. Time depends on what you need and when you need it. You can be assured however, that you can always pop that bad boy back in the oven and the flavor is maintained.

Hunger is a gift of priority.
It is felt. It is addressed.
No analysis or doubts are required.
Do not accept morsels when a meal is desired.
Craving is a delicious motivation.

Nourishment is achieved in many ways through many means.

Food for thought or food for soul or simply sustenance.

This dish is garnished with blessings.

Be sure to give thanks.

Most importantly, regardless of shape, ingredients or time…
You must decide the place

and people you wish to share this masterpiece with.

HOWL | Charles Dalton Telschow

When the echoes of your neighborhood fall silent, and the wind chimes stop ringing,

Breathe.

There is a time for inhalations and exultations.

Do not forget we are living in history, please make your contribution to the textbooks thoughtfully.

Scribble in the margins of love and hangman's noises and spirals that go all the way past the page, and remember the process of history that has brought that page into your presence. The tree that fell and was peeled layer by layer and chemically repurposed, to hold your thoughts for you. The weight of its death as it holds the heaviest of your breaths.

And your breath is so heavy these days. So heave it towards the moon and howl because it's 8 PM, and this is Denver. We are the echoes that do not fall silent, the porchlight that does not burn out, the PBR that stays cold, even in direct sunlight.

So carve your truth into the former flesh of your lungs, but do not think it is any truer than the air you would breathe because of these pages.

How generous of the trees to give us air, just so we can cut them down and write about how beautiful they were. How selfish of us to not tell of how disgusting we were to the beauty of this world. How dare we rewrite the history of our horrors until it shines, but can't see ourselves in it any more. Hoarding the grace under generic gentrified graffiti, and masks that do nothing to hide the fear in our eyes.

Remember the imperfection of tree branches, and how they worry not of straight lines and sterile wounds.

When the echoes of your neighborhood fall silent, and the wind chimes stop ringing,

Breathe in.

And howl.

Bread in the air | Ashley Howell Bunn

the greatest thing about dishes in the sink is that we have dishes and we have a sink and that I get to wash them when they get crusty and I hate that but there was food enough to be left behind and fungus enough in the air to make the dough rise and that you ate it with butter just like a victorian orphan and we laughed and then all played cards at the table and the greatest thing about the hole in the wall is that it is there and my hand made it and that there was emotion enough to propel it forward and that we are still here in this house and art sometimes covers the hole and sometimes it doesn't and one time you put your little shoe in the hole never to be seen again and I laughed and I found some old shoes to put on your feet and the greatest thing about that moment is that you have shoes and you have feet

Eve | Amy Wray Irish

When I reach to select the fruit
appearing most plump and ripe
my thumb plunges in, straight through
skin, meat, seeds, core
until it meets my fingers
creating a perfect circle.

Its all beautiful pulp in my palm.
No mold or rot here. I hold
a handful of sweet stickiness,
a shock of soft flesh. The surprise
forces a small *ha* of breath
to escape me, a moment of delight
that I then extend to you.

Not as temptation. More
as proof. Reflexively, instinctively,
I share this sensation
and offer you connection—
thinking that we share a rib,
a mythology. Any knowledge
for or against this is a fruit
I have yet to bite.

Ripe Apples | Jessica Rigney

You make of me a magician—
a laborer supplicant and servant
as I bring the corners of the cloth

together and know you see—
know of your marveling at my hands and
how they come together. It is I

who fashions a new heart each morning
awake to ripe apples which appear
inside the curve of my arm as though

I'd gathered them in my sleep.
Reveries write themselves upon the day
I say. Prefiguring every kindness falling

at my feet. By night they are siphon
for the sorrow tonguing my boots.
You make of me a witness—

stalwart bearer of deprivations
of sleep as I peel carrots at midnight
and know your eyes follow the line

of my shoulder to elbow to wrist and
how they work together still. It is you
who with your arms unloosening

'round the waste of me lost beyond
these endless unnamed days—you
who magics the seasons back from before

the stay.
Name not I, but the it which is this.
I say.

Hunger | Christopher Woods

Reading it for the third time, I am still amazed. Hungry, after midnight, in a hotel room in Galveston, I scan the room service menu in my lap. There, under the "Omelets" heading, it states that all are served with warm biscuits and yes, with mourning potatoes.

I am astounded. But I am also a realist and do not believe that biscuits will climb five floors and arrive still warm at my door. That they arrive at all is sufficient. Still, it distresses me to know that I have, for all this time, through all kinds of culinary weather, never known that some potatoes, by design or scheme or recipe, are meant only for mourning. I have eaten potatoes in all kinds of moods, even outside my homeland, and never, I think, funereally.

But I am also starving. I pick up the phone and call room service, order the potatoes without question, in an almost normal voice. Then, waiting in the dark, I hear waves crash against the seawall. The world is such an eerie place, I think, each day stranger than the one before.

Somewhere in the bowels of this hotel a room service cart is rolling this way, and for an instant I do not care if even death comes riding on it.

A Winter's Night | Varinia Rodriguez

I have learned to walk on fire,
To drink fire,
To be fire.

Half goddess,
Half dragon.

I am Medusa,
Bruja,
Y santa.

Give me your eyes,
I will teach you to read skins.
Give me your hands,
I will teach you to pray in tongues.

The night we met,
The moon bowed down
To give us the stars.

I watched women
Drape themselves
Onto you.

A production
In the art
Of meat dangling.

But there was your stare—
Unwavering,
On me
In reverence and lust.

I put my claw to your skin.

There is a power when the flame burns white between us.
Where the unholy meet
And give us light.

YUM | Caito Foster

I couldn't eat enough to fill myself,
an insatiable void,
and so I go hungry instead
to conserve resources
for the people I love

I'm not hungry anymore
I've got no more appetite for
my own suffering today,
I've got no tolerance
for the hunger pains,

I can feel them in my brain now,
vacant motel in my gut, flooded
I couldn't consume enough to
silence the deafening growling,
I can't tell where it's coming from,

I tried to starve my ego just in case,
turns out, it doesn't take a feast
to have us feeling full, in fact
the food is just a facade

I can't stop eating
anything that tastes like solidarity,
I can't stop wandering desolate grocery stores
in search of a flavor only found in the
soft palate of a girl I kissed in high school

She doesn't exist anymore
the sensation on my lips is just an

imagination figment, a fragment,
of a recipe long expired,

I'm not starving for my own
destruction anymore.
My mind would separate and
have me consume myself
down to bare bone, if it could,

Just so you could see
me for what I am,
a skeleton full of closets
coming out slowly,
patience running thinner,
says it's time for dinner.

None of That | Anna Leahy

A friend, a fellow poet, announces
that he will someday open a restaurant
called *None Of That*,
wanting customers to say
Oh, I'll have none of that,
and by *that*, he means *cheese*!

What confidence!
I see now, only years later,
its acronym: *NOT*.
I am jealous of his utter disdain.
I am jealous of his unwavering voice.
What would I not serve?
What would I not allow on my menu?

All I can think is beets,
but who likes beets?
They would not be missed.
No, I long to loathe
what others likely love,
and to be okay with that loathing.
But I am poor at decisions.
Insouciance is an illusion.

I desire to deny others
based on my own predilections,
the strength of my convictions,
whether right or wrong,
but I find myself lacking,
full of wishy-washy sympathy.
Though I don't much like—what?

what is it?—mint! trigger of my migraines,
I see how others might.
I have seen the thick tongue licking
mint-chocolate-chip from a cone,
have heard talk of julep, a spoonful of sugar
to help the medicine go down.

This friend will not stop.
He claims that his second restaurant will be called
None of That Either.
He has more, more than I can muster.
I try harder to think of something, *the* thing.
But all I want to keep from others
is what I most want for myself
because there might not be enough
to go around.

Pretzels | Danny Mazur

Every night before bed
I would wander into my Dad's kingdom
Laying on his king-sized bed
With a book and pretzels scattered across his hairy chest
His trusted steeds (10 lb. twin toy poodles)
Intently waited for treats
A low static from AM talk radio filled the room
He removed suit and tie
Donning blue converse shorts, no shirt

I remember the way his toes would wiggle
How he would tell me what he was reading about
How crumbs would fall from his lips
As he laughed at his own jokes

My mind was much quieter then
No concerns of burning forests or abused children
I wasn't stressed
By the weight of earning paychecks and paying off loans
I didn't find myself overwhelmed
How my dreams often feel like the Amazon River
7 miles wide
And I'm on the bank
I can't swim and my boat is on the other side

On good days,
I'll remember the world isn't about me
That dreams come and go
That I live with my best friend

In some sort of Earth fort
That I get to walk to work
And spend my days with kids

And when the night comes
I lay in my bed and give thanks to tired legs
I open a comic book and my toes begin to wiggle
It's in these moments
I find my hairy chest full of pretzels

The Sound of One Howl Howling | Roseanna Frechette

To hear the close distance,
your howl, when unable to find
one cold sliver of moon.

I opened warm window.
This frozen stuck body of me
shifting over to what it must be
in a house made of worry
and flammable things.

When survival is one hungry beast
lighting fires fast as
bear claws unleashed
in this box of a house, any house,
to find food, any food, feed
that soul hungry beast
eating sliver of moon
cooling fire on face of a moment
of hard-assed especially sweet stuff, any life.

I listen for line to connection.
Hear hot pulse of warm blood,
surprisingly bright, bursting
through like great wolf
shedding cloak of sheep's clothing
is this, yawping call I can't see, only feel
coming back like a boomerang self
to wild safety, close distance,
raw sound of one howl howling now.

I feared I was a werewolf | Jericho Hockett

failed,   feral at best,
stuck between   phases of moon,
my body out   of sync with time.
I was   promised bliss
with one bite,   but still I lie

abed in honey   phlox, sleepless,
joints aching   to be shredded,
skin to burst   as March ides
march on to   May's full flower
moon and past.   I passed

for human,   despite my howl,
the blood   curse,
even growling,   lacking only
fur, claws, sharp   teeth. Reserved
in every form   except of judgment

for what I thought   a werewolf
ought to be: a wound at best.
But the worst   feature was
my abject desire   to preserve
human remains.   Until I met

my werewolf's ghost   carrying scent
fresh human flesh   on spring breezes,
in gradual degrees   shifting my
dimensions   under all moons,
full,   dark.

The Motherfuckin' Broccoli | Irina Bogomolova

When your generalized anxiety disorder
looks like buying broccoli from your local Sprouts.

I walk in
phone in hand
in the case I forget my short list of three items
because you see this is a short trip
an
in and out trip
a
there's nothing we gotta stress about here trip
don't even need to freak out about the shopping cart cuz
it's a grab a basket kinda trip
so

I grab a basket
but only after
I grab some toilet paper
not on the list but I promise me
I'll thank me later
see,
we have
chicken, broccoli, milk, and dry shampoo if I can find it
but I can't find it
so we have chicken, broccoli, milk,
plus some toilet paper.

Chickens first, thin cut thighs
can't ever buy the first item so I grab the one from behind
I think this is how my mother raised me

or this is OCD
I guess it doesn't really matter
as I make my way to the broccoli
but find

it's not alone
so I grab the bag above its resting home
do it slowly like I'm busy
and she's digging through the broccoli
and I watch her, wonder
what are her standards to choosing?
and have I ever been doing it right?

but I don't want to impede
so I make way to the apples
pick four
but not the best kind
notice the last one is bruised
but god damn, if I overstay my visit
so I make my way back

but the broccoli
is a fucking social butterfly
whispering sweet nothings into someone else's ear
and this is round two
and I want nothing more than to disappear

so I make my way to the milk
knowing damn well this is the last item on the list
cuz you see this is a short trip

a no stress strip
a basket trip

so I get a half gallon
can't drag around the real thing kinda trip

then go back for round three
but damn
the mother fucking broccoli
has a hell of a problem with lonely

so I grab the bag above its resting place
do it slowly like I'm busy
and I watch him, wonder
what are his standards to choosing?
and have I ever been doing it right?

as I take my sweet time
and a window emerges
like God,
is parting the broccoli seas
saying it's finally got some time for me and I take it
pick one,
then two
and that's all I need
but then I notice her
take a bag from above the broccoli trees

and I stick around
want to see how other people deal
with the broccoli throw-down

so I dig for more
and she swoops in
like a real broccoli VIP

doesn't even look at me
digs through all the broccoli trees

and I pick a third one
though I don't need to
and when I look back on that moment I swear I got only
stem

learn later
that's actually the broccoli standard

you want less tree truck and more leaves
but I paid for tree trunk anxieties
as I concluded my
broccoli shopping spree
carried the bags in
but then skipped the meal
to jot this poetry

and isn't that how always it goes?
starving artists
finding everything as prose.

On My Mother's Birthday (1928–2018) | David Zaworski

As I think through my cooking today—
prep, seasoning, timing—
I think about you.

You taught me to measure, leveling off,
How to read a recipe (little t is not the same as big T)

You must have kept a bit of an eye out,
but I don't recall it, just guidance when asked,
certainly no hovering, great tolerance for failures

and of course your own cooking
modeling confident experimentation
both with and beyond recipes.

Off at college, Jim and I bought fresh green beans
then called you, long-distance rates back then,
asking how to cook them and were answered with
… a pause … and your gentle query,
"I think I sent a cook book with you?"

Now as I taste check the pot simmering
dried beans with onion, carrot, garlic,
mushrooms, smoky chili, herbs
—everything eyeballed, scooped,
pinched or dashed together—

now as I cook on this day,
the tears well up again
thankful and sad,
blessed beyond measure.

Say a Mass for Me Today | Daniel G. Snethen

Say a mass for me today.
If you do, it might
make a difference.
How will you ever know?

In sooth, if you don't say
a mass for me today, the world
will likely continue on
and most probably, so too will I.

But what if I die unexpectedly,
how will you feel then?
Will you wonder if a mass
would have made the difference?
Would a mass have stayed
my finger from pulling the trigger?

Would a mass have caused me
to stumble before stepping
onto the chair, thwarting my attempt
to place the loop around my neck?

If you say a mass for me today,
you may never know the difference
this act made for me. But if you don't,
you may one day wonder, what if?

So please Anne, do whatever it is
a good Catholic woman does
and say a mass for me today.

Gently touch every bead
for your bearded behemoth
and remember, it has been appointed
unto all men once to die—
even for a behemoth such as I.

Death is most definitely imminent,
but the actual time and day is an uncertainty.
Please Anne, make a difference.
and say a mass for me today.

Postal Distancing | Steve Shultz

I am essential.
I do not feel so.
I feel vulnerable,
open to attack.

I walk into the post office
Report for duty
Try to count my blessings
on my fingers before I
stuff them into nitrile gloves

I see all the clerks & carriers
with masks on

I collect my parcels, go to my case
all while telling myself I'm safe
(I do not feel safe)

Sorting mail
I am occupied
as my anxiety rises

I spray down my work space
& my truck with bleach
I try to wear a mask, but
I cannot breathe

I get out of my truck to
bring a parcel to a door

A woman stops me

That's fine right there

Her rubber-gloved hands
Lysol spray boxes from
Amazon's previous delivery

Back on my route
kids have drawn messages in chalk
beneath the mailboxes

♥ , Please Be Safe
(I do not feel safe)

Man approaches me
at stop 6, section 4
I'm almost done with my
deliveries for the day

The mailbox doors
are wide open as I begin
putting the letters & parcels
in their proper places

He parks his red pickup truck
a ways from the mailbox unit
Much more than 6 feet away
from me, I think to myself

He walks past me to a trash can,
disposes of some trash
He walks back, stands closer to me
(two feet away is my guess)

He wears a bandana
around his mouth & nose
His hands are gloved
He's wearing shorts although it's cold

I stand naked before him—
no mask around my face

Hey, I just want to check my mail, he says...
I'm at number something something something

Hey, I say, do you mind coming back
in a few minutes? I'm just getting started.
Is that cool?

He steps back, wounded,
but flashes me a thumbs up
Fucks off back to his truck

I am briefly left alone with his mail & my thoughts

Some customers really care
One is even my friend
He says, Hey man, are you OK?

I tell him I'm just stressed
He says, if I need anything
to please let him know

I finish my route, go home & take a shower
Keeping my distance from my family

Believing in a Troubled God | Bill Gainer

We Pray on Wednesday.
The same night they pull
the lotto.

The rest of the week
at the dinner table
we make wishes
for something better.

When Wednesday comes
we pray –
our wishes come
true.

On Thursday
we make wishes.

Hunger is an Excellent Cook | Brendan Hamilton

"Hunger is an Excellent Cook" is a collage poem composed from a variety of first person accounts from Civil War veterans describing food and beverages they encountered during their wartime experiences.
        -Captain John Henry Otto, 21st Wisconsin Infantry

Shin bone marrow,
razor-back hog,
nicely fried crackers,
worm sandwiches,
ash-cakes, Johnny cakes,
elastic pies, sewed or pegged,
peanuts still clinging to the vines,
raw bacon,
desecrated vegetables,
alleged soup,
evaporated silage with a trace of flies,
slapjacks, flapjacks
tough as a mule's ear,
concrete breakfast slab,
mush and dumplings,
dish of dunderfunk,
sloppy, slimy Yankee beans,
imitation coffee made of parched wheat rye,
genuine "Lincoln" coffee,
sugar raw, by handfuls,
delicate flesh of barnyard fowls,
mulberries, dead ripe,
green, knotty apples,
a gaunt old Arkansas steer,
sassafras buds,
sausages and hominy,

coarse cow peas,
canned lobsters,
hogshead molasses,
woodshed molasses,
persimmon brandy,
spiritus frumenti,
stumptail beer swill,
canteens full of home-made whisky,
whisky so mean you could taste the boy's feet who
plowed the corn.
mud suckers and turtles,
Kentucky apple-jack,
Louisiana rum, hot from the still,
mussels, fried, stewed, boiled, and baked,
pieces of rat,
cold corn dodgers,
corn meal bread, corn meal coffee, corn meal soup,
corn pudding, corn pie, corn pone,
raw, shelled corn,
parched acorns,
blue beef,
cup of flour and a chunk of horseflesh
boiled on an old tin plate,
unbolted flour, kneaded into a dough, wound
around iron ramrods
held over the fire.

Untitled | Sarah LaRue

A spider
landed somehow in my
bathroom trash basket,
dancing frantically among tissues.
I told her in a singsong voice
I wanted freedom for her,
lowering a short glass with folded paper
angling to evacuate.

She found corners of the bag inside
and skittered to climb the crinkling plastic
exhausted then retreating to a fold.
I urged her on a minute longer then scoffed
some creatures might just rather die—
maybe more prefer a death they know
to a life they don't.

Later I came back to see her still
trying, dancing, hiding—
if the only hands you see offering
help look like the same ones that hurt you
help gets hard to hold.

I turned the basket over
out on the front stoop
She dizzied spun around then
righted herself to run.

Freedom demands some undoing.
Not every victory can look you in the eye.
Done (Free) can be enough.

License Plates on the Barn Wall | Guinotte Wise

Some Hawaii that say *Aloha* from back in the days we island-hopped MidPac Air with work in hand for Westin Hotels and various businesses. We flew standby, hardly ever missed a flight. Once, we took the trimaran from Maui to The Big Island and the hotel manager brought people, box lunches with champagne aboard. Turtles swam alongside as in a blue dream. Kansas plates, lots of them, Missouri, too. California motorcycle plates, small for the big Harley, big plates for the black Caddy with black windows, a special model with little chrome. Then old plates before our time, low numbers, fewer people on the road, a farmer finger waving from the wheel, he spits into a Folger's can. That New Mexico plate with Zia says Land of Enchantment and that's especially true during Indian Market in Santa Fe and my great uncle's ghost wanders Taos with paint brushes and a faint odor of turpentine. These plates form a tapestry of colors and memories, unfaded Kodachromes of such wing shot, quick passing moments and so indelible as they swim up shimmering in the developer pan, look! says a 1966 plate remember the twist? Remember partying all night and running out of cigarettes and things better left unsaid? A bullet hole in the ceiling, a lumpen form sleeping in the

cold on the front lawn. Let him be, wasn't
invited anyway. The Husky watches him.
Jack had a Jaguar XK140 and before that
Mussolini's son's Alfa Romeo Legerra
with right hand drive and sweeping lines.
Jim Pike rode that Triumph Bonneville
and raced Goldstars on the coasts, I left a
BSA in Omaha in pieces, fled to Aspen,
cannonballed in everything, recklessly,
but lived and rode into the Superstitions
with a wife-to-be, she found more gold
than I, then Jazz in the Woods, then that
long drive to Los Angeles, still looking
for gold, found some flakes out there but
none to assay, then I thought why not look
for the actual stuff, not the metaphor, and
panned for it in the Sierra Nevada, in the
icy cold snow melt of the Yuba River. Only
found a little peace, some trout we cooked
in an iron skillet with some bacon, lemon.
The license plates from Wisconsin, Iowa,
not worth keeping, no peace, and memory
is a liar. Kansas again, Missouri too. Years
ran like Usain Bolt and my own dad who
almost caught up with Jesse Owens' time.
Oh, the dogs, the times, the horses, fast
motorcycles, cars and possibilities, those
the futuramas offered to us in dreams of
wealth and never growing old. Suddenly
we did. When's the wealthy part kick in?

Yeggman Blues | Catfish McDaris

A million pesos in confetti in the wind,
She said, "I don't care if you're a hot shot
safe cracker don't stare at my dog too long."

"Or what?"

"You'll regret it."

That night Porterhouse must've stared too
long, by morning he'd turned into a tumble-
weed rolling south toward Mexico.

Pandemic Escapees | Leah Mueller

Lying in our motel bed
halfway between
Washington and Arizona:

fitful crossroads
of a dirty central
California town.

Steinbeck country
minus the romance.

Days Inn of Westley,
ground-floor room
with a parking lot view,
68 dollars plus tax.

I shove my ears tight
against the pillows
to stifle the endless
rumble of semis.

Dreams punctuated
by the frantic
shriek of brakes
and the sudden roar
of acceleration.
Truckers cannot
afford to rest,
and neither can we.

Tomorrow night,
the two of us
will reach Joshua Tree
and sleep in the room
where Gram Parsons died.

In the morning,
we will have breakfast
on the patio, seated alone
in gritty iron chairs

beside the artificial
blue shimmer
of a swimming pool:

your gaunt cheeks pale
as you scoop food
from its Styrofoam wrappings.

So far to drive until
the desert appears.

So much in the
rearview mirror, getting
smaller by the second.

Nothing is the Other's Blinding | Liam Max Kelley

I am gagging up axioms
after one too many
trips to the refrigerator—

fire is no place for a fall,
    ethic is phony if left
        outside for too long,
            nothing is the other's blinding—

I am disinfecting these words again,
scarring at the back of the throat,
and wanting more space to breathe—

life breaks and gorges desert-like,
    food cannot grieve in an ocean,
        hunger for itself gets wet in the mouth
            at the thought of all these trapped souls,
                morning stops feeling heavenly

        (like a fool with fingers stuck
            to the burning stovetop).

I am loathing to compass the devil
by the collar and demand payment
for time lost rubbing my hands
together, waiting for the rest
of my body to get the hint—
to loan him my shirt and short shorts,
my black socks and Brylcreem,
and tell him to fall down
over and over again.

I am still rubbing the surface
of this puke-filled floor—

people get their cut of the pot,
   close up of chin hair from time to time,
      jetstream chance is something to do—

    (like greasy magnet residue on
      the metal icebox).

I am sagging under
the belly weight
of bottles I bought
when I shouldn't have gone out.

Thou Shalt Not Lock the Fucking Door | Matt Clifford

Food - here's a thought: you need it, it's yours. And if someone tries to stop you we will look in their dumpster. If their dumpster is full then so are we all. If it's empty we will ask what they need. If their dumpster is locked, we will write give us this day with the blood of their empty heart. Get that bread.

Thou shalt not lock the fucking door.

Our daddy, give us this day.
Give it to us, father.
We will take it.
One way or another.
I'm going to feed you.
Going to find food.
If we need to we'll eat you.

That shit is everywhere. There's more than enough of it finally. Evolution hasn't caught up to such excess. We are running scarce storing up fat and sugar stockpiling essential futures like the end of the world depends on them. We are tired but we made it. We don't have to make anymore. You will make more than you did yesterday. You will eat the same amount. You will wash your neighbors' dishes. You will buy more dishes. How clean do you think we can make this planet?

I keep tidy my corner of the dumpster. When they are done with me I ask for more work. There is an ache in my stomach and a spring in my soul that is demanding material for developing fire. I chop wood like I did before enlightenment and trade it to the papermaker who sells it back to the poet in me to print the words for them to burn so I have something to cook my dinner over. I will sweep the ashes up after we finish, let them just relax.

I know this great toilet across town I think you'd really like.

It's a fine spot to think.

This is not the cool dystopia I was promised | Lonnie MF Allen

This is not the cool dystopia I was promised.

I thought there'd be neon lit night skies with
rain beautifully coming down on trench coats.
Instead there are annual floods along the gulf
displacing the poorest.

I thought there'd be nanobots
spying on us disguised as insect swarms.
Instead there are invasive murder hornets
and let's be honest
we are all willingly spied on
with a click of a button.

I thought there'd be sentient robots uprisings
and they'd be exterminating humans.
Instead, robots in an Amazon factory
help workers fall to their death
and no one helps
because they're told to get back to work
by humans.

This is not the cool dystopia I was promised.

I thought contagious zombies would attack us all
and the government would vainly send out the military.
Instead we get a highly contagious virus
and the government says get back to work!

I thought our president would be part of the illuminati
or some other secret society
instead we have a moron
who constantly thinks the government
whom he leads is conspiring against him.

I thought we'd be out in the desert
with spiked shoulder pads fighting for gas.
Instead we can't stop pumping and fracking
and pumping and fracking.
Ka chunk Ka chunk Ka chunk
no matter what the cost.

This is not the cool dystopia I was promised.

I thought there'd be aliens attacking us from Planet 9
And we'd all fight united against them.
Instead we have COVID-19
that disproportionately affects black people.

I thought the internet would be a virtual reality
where we'd fight against an evil sentient AI.
Instead it's a place where racism, misogyny,
and all around hatred are shared by us.
I thought the dark web would be where the rebellion starts
Instead it is the place of child sex trafficking.

This is not the cool dystopia I was promised.

I thought there'd be roaming bandits and lawlessness.
It would be the law of the jungle out there!
Instead police officers and vigilantes gun down

innocent black boys
who still wait for justice.

It's not fair.
I bought all those guns.
I built that bomb shelter.
I have all that canned food.

And this is the way the world ends?
Not with a bang, but with no toilet paper?

Toilet Paper Blues | Jane Ripley

You want a roll?
I can get you a roll.
I can get you a roll by 4:20 p.m. in April.
It's better than Pine Cone Christmas bud man!
Brothers and Sisters—
I got DAKINE!
One sheet, industrial,
Scratchy-ass, cardboard cylinder in da middle.
Will satisfy about 200 goes.
You need a roll?
I work with rolls.
Last week at work
My boss and I got the last box
In the county.
Man, this shit is GOLD.
I could probably sell it on the black market for,
Say 10,000 dollars a roll.
Damn, never in my wildest fantasies
Did I ever think t.p.
Would be the go-to thing.
The new trend.
Hot commodity,
The Shiz—
Anything
To wipe that shit
That sticks to your ass
And the paper

Rolls into little dingleberries
That hangs from your butt-hairs.
Yes, that's what people want most.

Holy shite!
It's not about Chai tea
Not about French Fries
Not about Prime Ministers
Or whether to vape or smoke cigarettes.
It's all about the immortal,
Unstoppable, never-ending roll!
Like Jack Kerouac's novel
"On the Road"
Where he just kept typing and typing.
That DUDE was ahead of his time.
HE had a roll!
You want a roll?
I got ROLLS baby!
Soft and Chumley's
And Taciturn and obsequious.
Rolls and rolls and rolls and rolls.
Rolls for St. Patrick's Day.
Kelly Green!
Rolls for Christmas
And rolls for Halloween!
I got rolls you aint gonna get
Anywhere else.

I got rolls but I'm in lockdown mode
So pick 'em up on Ebay!
Along with Arrow Brand Elf
Disinfecting red wipes with flowers by the pound.
You want a roll?
I got your rolls!
I GOT YOUR ROLLS!!!

Virtual Easter | Jennifer Faylor

Up at seven flat for online Easter mass
pour Irish cream into instant coffee
as the archbishop jokes to vacant pews
of his mother at home drinking a Bloody Mary
he speaks of emptiness & fullness
later I text photographic evidence
of stress-baked blueberry cinnamon rolls
to a friend quarantined in Queens
it would have been more fitting
to use yeast and let them rise
but the stores were sold out

Drunk at King Soopers | Jonathan Bluebird Montgomery

Back in my more lost days I'd have a few Jack&Cokes and go to the grocery store. The drinking was for other social reasons, but in the midst of my buzz I'd remember there was no food at home and something hadta be done. It was usually after midnight, so I'd hafta go to King Soopers, which at the time was open 24 hours.

When I went to the supermarket sober I'd second guess myself out of everything. I'd see it all causing fat or irritable bowel syndrome or out-of-money. Even the potatoes, even the toilet paper, even the novels of Dean Koontz. But going in drunk I magically forgot all that and got whatever the hell I wanted…

Cookie Crisp cereal. Chips Ahoy (chewy). And Ben&Jerry's Chocolate Chip Cookie Dough ice cream.

Raisin Bran Crunch. Ben&Jerry's Coffee Toffee Crunch. And Nestle Crunch Bar.

Frosted Flakes. Frosted Mini-Wheats. And straight up can of frosting.

Cheese and Pepperoni Bagel Bites. Stouffer's French Bread Pepperoni Pizza. And Pepperoni Pizza Hot Pockets.

A huge jar of Jiff peanut butter. A huge jar of Vlasic bread and butter chip pickles. And huge jar of Red Vine licorice.

King's Hawaiian Sweet Rolls. 128 oz Hawaiian Punch (with the handle). And a big spikey-top pineapple.

Dr. Pepper 24-pack. Pepperidge Farm Geneva cookies. And creamy pink Pepto Bismol.

Trix. Birthday balloons. And a fresh bouquet of rainbow colored flowers.

A steak knife. Matches. And a novel by best-selling author Dean Koontz.

Oh yeah, I'd be skipping thru the aisles and nodding at all the stockers. I'd strike up a conversation with the guy monitoring the automatic self-checkouts.

"What's up, man!" I'd say loudly.

"Not much," he'd say quietly.

One time I remember emptying my cart and scanning all the items' barcodes over the laser and suddenly realizing there was one thing I hadn't gotten yet. A thing that really mattered. A thing that was really obvious.

But I was too drunk to remember what that one thing was.

I scanned my mind for the answer, but the only words I could find were "drunky-dunky-doo!"

I rummaged through my items, hoping maybe I'd actually already gotten The One Thing. There was so much stuff, a bounty of nourishment and supplies. But it was just not there. It was indifferent to how badly I needed it.

"Incomplete groceries!" I yelled at it.

The self-checkout supervisor heard and came over.

"What's the problem?" he said. "Did it freeze up on you?"

"Yeah," I said, "the brain part did."

Then he got out his little electronic card, which could fix all the problems of the checkout, and swiped it.

"Seems like it's working," he said.

"No," I said, "nothing works without The One Thing."

"I don't know what that is tho."

I noticed the eye bags and slump shoulders and colorless skin of his graveyard shift body. Then I looked over at all the shit I was trying to buy.

"Look, man," I said. "Can I just put this back?"

"You don't want it now?"

"What's the point?"

"Okay," he sighed, "I'll put it back for you."

"No, don't do that. It's my fault for getting the shit out."

"It doesn't bother me. I'll do it."

"Okay, I'm sorry."

"It's okay."

"I'm drunk and can't remember The One Thing."

"I know."

Then I just shrugged and stumbled out the automatic door too ashamed to look back.

Today, I'm not as lost and usually only go to the store midday and clear-headed and get the same few things that seem most important.

Classic-yellow box Cheerios. Gallon jugs of El Dorado Spring Water. And whatever brand of hand soap happens to be on sale.

I still can't remember The One Thing.
But like several Jack&Cokes a night, I guess I'll just go on without it.

Dick Dale Cures the 'Rona | Shawn Pavey
    for Jason Vivone

Let's just say you had a meltdown in the grocery store
because your hands are so dry from washing and
sanitizing
that you can't open the plastic produce bags
and your glasses are fogging up from your own breath

escaping through the top of your quickly fashioned
quarantine mask constructed from cut out swaths
of an old trade-show t-shirt and elastic hair ties
and there's no toilet paper on the shelves

and they're out of the brand of toothpaste
that has kept you cavity-free since college
which, now, was more than thirty goddamned
years ago. Let's say you had that meltdown.

Let's say it's late afternoon on a Thursday
and even though you should be working from home
this trip to the grocery store is the closest thing you've had
to a vacation all fucking year and there's no real work
anyway

and after parking the car, sanitizing the groceries,
putting the groceries away, and realizing that your
very public and, now, embarrassing meltdown
is going to eat at you for weeks, for months (let's be real,
years),

you turn on the radio and your guitar teacher

who is also a part-time DJ
on a local listener-supported station
starts playing *Miserlou* and, later, *Pipeline* by Dick Dale
and the magic of Fender spring reverb tanks and single-
coil pickups

cures the Coronavirus blues.

How to Slice Open an Avocado | Rosemerry Wahtola Trommer

After cutting open hundreds, thousands
of avocados, I marvel as my friend Kyra
cuts off the top. Slices it right off.
And I stare at her, at the knife, at the tip
of the avocado listing on the cutting board.
How easily she scoops out the creamy green flesh.
How simply she cuts more rounds around the pit.

All these years, I've sliced avocados lengthwise.
It's as if I've just learned a new word for yes.
As if the sun itself just rose right here in the kitchen.
It takes so little to open us, to help us
see everything new. Even that prayer I pray
the same way. These hands. This common fruit.

On the Trail | Michael Sage

Releasing the pent-up quarantine's wail
from a loathsome shelter tank,
we thirsted for energy at river's trail,
trading currency in nature's bank.

South Platte has gifted refuge before:
when placer's gold beckoned stage one.
Native memories long defined its shores
where Arapahos danced under the sun.

Now all subject to intractable bind
wrought by the virus at hand,
a rigorous trial attacking body and mind,
only our soul can meet the demand.

There is but one natural escape
where thoughts bounce off water's gleam,
to reflect without choice on our collective fate
while traversing from factory to stream.

Outside the bank vulnerability cries,
as the Elders have a message to send:
respect the space where danger lies,
our tribulations will eventually suspend.

But vulnerability has a peculiar hue
where disconnection births an anxious cry,
protest gathers upon a dangerous cue
while the hands of fate multiply.

Yet I noticed beauty even amidst the grief,
before quarantine swallowed the whole of day.

As prudence waits for summer's relief
a serene picture can also allay.

Geese climbing the bank without fear,
as the hiker embarks from mountain's base,
while goslings at side they hold ever dear,
'tis no longer a desperate chase.

Ducks swimming and fishing as they please,
in fresh water from seasonal snows,
as the hawk swoops down right over their beaks,
disturbing ripples from the water's flow.

We know sudden disturbance as well,
of viral reaction and expanding wake,
and like the ducks who stood bravely through the swell
our soul will strengthen on the uptake.

Nature has seen such convulsions before
in a history of ages gone by,
the river's song continues this lore
for as long as the birds can fly.

One final message to circle this tale
from an ageless rhythm and rhyme:
a solemn melody to part with the trail,
though circle is broken only for a time.

Fate has disturbed a comfortable sound,
bringing the cacophonous challenge of our days,
let us turn this weary vinyl around
then pause before we play.

Mother nature will be there no matter our choice,
where her songs never skip the tracks.
The only question is whether we hear her voice
… and its call to welcome us back.

SEA | Umar Nizar

Suffocated somewhere
Within the depths of the blues
Was Noah's ark.
The souls aboard
Bubbled out to the surface
Looked the sun straight in the eye
And caused the greenhouse effect.

is I'm not | Jake Riley

Always why always the urge to go
And live inside some cave alone
A place where one could go unknown
And live unsurveiled by the eye

That cares not if you sleep at home
Or camp out in the forest grove
And wake among the dirty pines—
Who cares not if you live   or die?

And what's the problem sweetie, with your weeping?
Is it really that that's what's keeping
Me from offshoots I'm off seeking
Toward our ever-closing door?

I might as well be a pair of boots
Kicking delicate glassworks to the floor
But really is it only that or is it really something more?

Observe: a hollow in me
A long, and even then longer hollow
And an EXIT arrow that I follow
Down that endless endless black black corridor

The truth is (of your weeping)
I don't feel anything
The real problem (is as always)
I don't feel anything
I love you (and you're beautiful)
I don't feel anything
Except a sense of shifting in the aforementioned floor

I can feel the boards beneath me circl ing up
Taking the boots, the calves, the knees
A third of me or more, gone, as if disease
Were filling from the bottom me, the ever empty cup

You say now would be the time to dance
And live as much of living as I can
And I would, should I be any other man
But the whole point of what I'm saying is I'm not

                        I'm sorry sweetie
                        For the weeping
                        is I'm not

    Being being broken
    Bears repeating
    is I'm not

                        And sorrier still
                        I must be leaving
                        is I'm not

it will not matter | Scout Noa Halpern

it will not matter
whose anxiety triggered whose
when we are both lying at the bottom of the ocean.

it will not matter
who's technically a hypochondriac
and who's technically on the spectrum
when the breath fueling words between us
is gone whether we like it or not.

it will not matter
how many times you try to escape this
this— this— this—
the floorboards stiffen when they feel your feet
wishing they were somewhere else,
like my spine,
when my body feels the spinning inside your head
churning up my chest
racing through my veins.

it will not matter
how well we lived in between glass dividers
for the last eleven months
when our heads are smashing against them,
shattering each others' illusions
of space and sanity.

it will not matter
when it's all over
but i am alive now.
i must be allowed to take deeper breaths

i must be allowed to cry
i must be allowed to scream, when it all caves in,
and when my world inevitably crumbles down,
it is not up to you.

Speak to Me | Emylee Frank

Speak to me.
Speak to me, ever so softly.
Like how the wind whispers
Through the flowers.
Pushing bees along the way,
For when their wings get heavy.

Speak to me.
Speak to me, ever so softly,
Like how the little waves of salty-goodness
Kiss the sand
And erase its memories.

Speak to me,
Speak to me, ever so loudly,
Like how the lightning brightens the sky
And the thunder screams at whoever is listening.

Speak to me,
Speak to me, please,
For I need guidance.
For I need direction.

Speak to me,
Speak to me please,
I feel lost and there is a fog
that has thickened
and draped itself over me.

Please speak to me,
Speak to me however way you feel

necessary,
as your voice is what
navigates me through this...

this storm.
This chaos and uncertainty.
Speak to me,
My darling, speak to me.

My toes balance on a tightrope,
I'm lost
between entropy and flourishing.

Trying to distinguish the difference
feels irrelevant.
What a hard pill that is to swallow.

Speak to me,
Speak to me ever so softly,
Let your words direct me to
close my eyes.
May your winds speak volumes into my
ears and push me

to let go
and soar with my heavy wings.
Just like the bees.

Darling, speak to me
so I can shine bright as lightning
and scream my accomplishments into the sky.

Darling, speak to me,

and tell me it is safe to release these memories.
To let the past drift out to sea.

Speak to me,
speak to me ever so softly
and please tell me I am home.

OCCUPY LOVE | Judyth Hill

Let the seeds fall
raspberry peony and Chinese poppy, that rattling word gourd.
Let the seeds of love cascade through you,
grow the heart of a fishmonger, a baker, a lily.

Occupy Love,
that space inside the skin of start.
Clap your hands three times,
make peace
with your sister, your neighbor, your memories.

Go and tell the bees.

Occupy Love. You are safe.
Let that be your story. Wake to a morning dizzy with cowbells,
purple rampion, forget-me-nots.
Breathe in this day, this glamour of now.

You are home.
Surrender and just be here
with every mistake and every chance and each breath,
until you are taken over, besieged,
a city, a country, a planet,
fallen to love.

Los saguaros are being destroyed | Marcy Rae Henry

        The sun is needed and also dangerous
   Beneath it people hide things for others
           en la sombra de saguaros

Water in containers painted black
        to absorb not reflect sun
  Sunscreen   Sombreros
        Clothes   Crude maps

Imagine the sun betraying your whereabouts
        Not using a phone for fear
     of becoming a little black
        dot crossing a line

        . . . .

   Oh sí, your location is being commodified

Along with cages and the cages around them

    The   virus   travels   like   the   rich

        Saguaros can die of frost
spreading over expandable skin and fruit red as royalty

  Wooden ribs can hold two hundred gallons of rain
Si se dejan al sol y la lluvia saguaros can live two centuries
    As long as this country has been
        Longer than this f r o n t e r a has been

     To kill or steal a saguaro is a felony

    Cactus cops who normalmente roam the border
now stand by while saguaros are removed
               to make room for a wall whose removal
                      will be reminiscent of Berlin

Después de cien años a saguaro starts to grow its first arm
    lifting it into the sky as if to say
Dame tus cansados tus pobres your huddled masses
yearning to breathe libres   Envíame los desposeidos
  I lift my lámpara beside the sun-colored door

What a Gift to be Born into Darkness | Kali Heals

What a gift to be born into darkness
Already dancing with discovery
Fingertip thin trust
A vulnerable pioneer of agency and comforts
In and out of reach

I offer my hand

Tension and release form sound
I could not tell if I felt or heard my heartbeat first
But it became the song in all

Synesthetic teachers
A whisper to the heavens
Who come back with thunder to wake
And rain to nurture

Let us sing together

A bird of paradise is not a malformed bird
But a flower whose petal-wing wind-whistle song
Harmonizes cricket-leg grass-blade
On grounds unseen, water still nurtures

Let us sing until our eyes adjust

Let us smile together
Let us cry together
Let us thank our mother together

This ravaged earth
Fearlessly compassionate
A wakeful candle in a golden dish
A torch flame honored to die out
Volcanic womb homage to
Impermanence and resurrection

We may be ash but we are also fire, water and earth, living and decaying
Divine integration

All-encompassing as love
As inescapable as nature
As available as we allow ourselves to be
Opposition shows the path
May we have breath enough to last

And if we do not, I still will
Graveyards could be gardens if we just stopped using boxes
Get out
Get out of your boxes
And let your eyes adjust

I offer my hand

Let It Be | Arlis Mongold

Once,
My house was on fire and I sat on the couch until the roof collapsed.

Later,
A nurse wiped tears from my melted ice cream face and said "I'm glad you made it."
Made it where, I wondered.

But mostly the nurses were quiet.
When you ingest too much horror, you sometimes lose words.

On Tuesday nights a singer-songwriter would visit.
A blonde with big teeth who would only strum Beatles songs.

"Let it Be" was her favorite.
As though she were telling me:

"That face of yours that looks like meatloaf sliding down a wall—let it be."

remembrance | Sarah Jane Justice

on the foreign tongue of memory,
our former homes taste sweet

bricks stay veiled in crystal ginger
green grass pleasantries never fade

in memory,

cracked wall truths are left to sweat
flame heat licks forgotten sores
until we can't ignore the blisters

This is a Test | Eli Whittington

This is a test
This is only a test
Had this been an actual disaster
The body count would be higher
Don't worry
This is only a
(inter)national emergency

This is only a test
Had this been an actual apocalypse
The store shelves would not be half full
The stations would be broadcasting
The advice of experts
And imbeciles

Had this been an actual emergency
Schools would be closed
Events would be cancelled
People would be scared

This is only a test
Of your resolve
Of your ability to aid community
Mutually

Had this been an actual emergency
Old growth forests would be burning
Species would be disappearing

In Chinese medicine,
Grief is stored in the lungs

Our collective lungs are burning
Our collective grief
Spreading
Like pandemic
Like panic
And this
Is only a test

Three Blue Apron Found Poems | s. Nicholas

adapting
Roasted Cauliflower Panzanella

remove sweetness
while small
while tender
while 2, 12, 20
you divide thinly your
core
separate, slice,
smash into pieces
until pierced
until break
until enough
and then you
discard

ancestor
Warm Grain Salad

dressed in orange your
favorite bright orange
dress beautiful orange coat

considered complete by many

still
to prevent the skin of your hands
from the rub
of this millennia
on paper on lined
paper on lined paper cutting
between the membranes and from
the membranes cut out
the segments the membranes
and toss into place pick each piece
gently and discard

thoroughly
Moo Shu Vegetables

turn aside most
delicate American traditions

root your core
to a small farm

create pliable time
working your fingers
over smooth green leaves
or brush through water

or
using matchsticks
at an angle loosely
(if you have reflected)
set this Southern/Northern
scene to separating

until it ends

To Melons | Gerard Sarnat

If were able to do it all again,
I'd pursue a Ph.D. in picking
sweet honeydews, cantaloupes
and watermelons—which skill
has eluded me for more than 7
revolting decades trying hard
as hell with little return
on investment.
               The first thing
after internet search, I would
identify primo produce outlet
for wo/men who have learned
from trial 'n error characteristics
that predict top-notch juiciness.
Since judging fruits by their rinds
hasn't worked
               I would apprentice
myself to observe if maybe squeezing,
sniffing umbilici, smelling the flesh,
texture during cutting, whether seeds
are desiccated, etc. in any way anticipate
how to select most tasty at the wholesale
market—then translate such techniques
into a reputation monetizing top quality.
But when Coachie
               attempted to incorporate the
above story into frame of this morning's
FaceTime reading Tales of Peter Rabbit,
struggling to perhaps help his Israeli son-in-law
shove more oatmeal and raspberries into Yanai
and Liav's mouths lippidy-lippidy just like

our bunny running to outpace Mr. McGregor;
I'm your abject failure in this sphere since oy!
kids simply begged Abba for casaba's
                nutrition-void sugar water.

For the Sad Waitress at the Diner in Barstow | Alexis Rhone Fancher

beyond the kitchen's swinging door,
beyond the order wheel and the pass-through piled
high with bacon, hash browns, biscuits and gravy,

past the radio, tuned to 101.5-FM
All Country - All the Time,
past the truckers overwhelming the counter,
all grab-ass and longing.

in the middle of morning rush you'll
catch her, in a wilted pink uniform,
coffee pot fused in her grip, staring over
the top of your head

you'll follow her gaze, out the fly-specked, plate
glass windows, past the parking lot,

watch as she eyes those 16-wheelers barreling
down the highway, their mud guards
adorned with chrome silhouettes of naked women
who look nothing like her.

the cruel sun throws her inertia in her face.
this is what regret looks like.

maybe she's searching for that hot day in August
when she first walked away from you.

there's a choking sound
a semi makes, when it pulls off the

highway; that downshift a death rattle
she's never gotten used to.

maybe she's looking for a way back.
maybe she's ready to come home.

(But for now) she's lost herself
between the register and the door, the endless
business from table to kitchen, she's

as much leftover as those sunny side eggs,
yolks hardening on your plate.

*First published in The San Pedro River Review, 2016

Belief | Taylor Jones

It's a human trick to impose meaning on everything

(the call of the owl
the pictures we draw in the stars).

Everything has to stand for something
everything has to be an omen
because we are too afraid to go out unprotected into the
wild whirling day.

I used to believe in luck
back when I believed in God
and thought prayer was just a candlelit petition for
      more
      more
      more.
Now I believe in
something accidental
that sometimes leaves me choking and twitching
senseless with
more.

I don't believe in karma.
I'm never going to pay
for all those bugs I stepped on as a kid
(though I used to stare at the garish cuts of beef at the
grocer's;
that could just as easily be me in there
neatly sectioned
mummified in saran wrap.
That's why I'm a vegetarian).

Being kind doesn't matter.
I want to be kind anyway.

Being joyful doesn't matter.
I want to be joyful anyway.

The world is beautiful and cruel.
Take the beauty. Grab as much as you can hold in both hands
and run.

I believe in miracles.
They are the right kind
of accident.

The kind you impose meaning on.

The kind you
steal.

Pepper | Jeff Burt

Blame my extravagant passion
      on the bread
toppling woven baskets, broken,
      pulled, dipped, shared,

or perhaps blame the turmeric and curry
      that wrap a jacket
over the rice like yellow sheets twisted
      over warm lovers,

or blame the pepper that emboldens
      my speech
to make things sing with an earnest joy
      like the sun-shower chirps

of small birds come to sift for small packets
      of seeds left by the last flowers,
the long red slice of pepper
      shaped like a clamp

that has seized my tongue and makes it run
      with stilted awkward speech
like a marionette in the hands
      of an invisible master.

the problem with talking love | Rebecca Hannigan

before walking into the courthouse i was eating bread
and a pastry that was supremely delicious and sweet and
tangy and
i was so happy, i feel so nasty now
and i think, going through security, that if for some reason
i had to work in this building, i'd open a bakery
but now, up to the third floor, we enter and
on one side of the room, we see those neo-Nazis

so my friend goes over and
tries to talk love - but my friend has long hair and
a chin that's all fuzz and the problem with
talking love is that it's easy after it's been accepted once
but the first time it's a pain and often
doesn't make it from one person to another, the other
won't hear it
or believe it or believe it's sincere

if anyone believes in Sincere
i know there are cliché ways to show love to strangers
but there's something about smiles that seem insulting,
the smiler is contemptuous, showing you pity,
they must be laughing so you laugh back
as a natural defense - the funny - a basic solvent,
universal scent, like garlic,

you're embarrassed when you think you should be, your
cheeks
know blushing, then you feign awareness,
preferring to be wrong and proud
than right and put down

i lean my head on my friend's shoulder
this friend preaching love who looks like a hippie, some say,
he must be crazy

but really, it's his lack of ego that's uncomfortable,
he doesn't primarily see himself
or give any fucks when he dresses in scarves and velvet skirts
and i feel like a jerk - a cynic - but at some point i've told him
i'm skeptical of everyone who's functional today
because nothing today is functioning
i mean

look at the court, Your Honor, these here, prosecuted,
one man at the podium, asking again and again, have i been
charged with Domestic Violence?

the Judge says, Sir, you should get your lawyer,
what you say is on the Public Record,
we're all on the Public Record,
we don't have lawyers
we can't wait

after a brief recess
my friend pictures the Judge with a kickball,
captain picking teams,
kids picked last, we're in the back
with the other activists and i'm sitting
i'm passive, i'm here
supporting my friend, who's supporting the activist,

really i'm just suggestible

really i'm just suggesting
as far as good goes
this girl against the fascists
my friend against the affluent
men and estrogen
oceans and effluent
effort and effortless, the Judge looks sleepy

the law is contingent upon your ability to pay for it
the activist we're here to support is up,
the Judge gives her a date and
we watch the neo-Nazis stand, until next time,
the jury needs coffee
my legs ache
i think of yeast
my friend says we should wait around
just in case, who's in charge
in trial and error, my friend smiles and
loves and loves and loves
and i hear someone laughing.

About My Breasts, Since You Asked | Sherre Vernon

In the Russian sauna, two
old women scrub me without
consent. Through the birch-branch
steam I avert my eyes, but there are bodies
everywhere. Just this once, breasts like mine:
thank god. thank god. thank god.

**

My breasts believe in Archimedes, float
above my sinking body. With the water, they are
full & well-positioned. My lover, the mathematician,
wonders why they can't be like this
always. At least there is something lovely
in the contrast of my nipples against my skin.

**

I thought *bosom* was a chest in *blossom*,
the vowel a sigh into adulthood, the *ah*
both breath & connection. How disappointing,
the words that actually find me—*badonka-donks*,
tig-ol-bitties—and keep me wishing
for other skin.

**

My classmates have decided the women
in the *National Geographic* must have
breasts like that for lack of underwire
or by nursing too many babies. Telling
them otherwise would expose me.

**

My mother sleeps prophetic & topless
her breasts an advertisement. How
could I know – what did I know of
shirts strangling themselves around us
in our sleep?

**

In order to breathe, girls like me, we
sleep in our bras. It's the closest we come
to sleek. In my twenties, for headstand,
an old man shows me how to strap myself in,
how to keep my boobs at bay.

**

I'm thirteen & the man at the counter calls me
thick, makes a sweet exhale through
the side of his mouth. Another hollers
an invitation from the street. A third pushes by,
his breath hot in my ear & on my face, his
body scraping into the cotton on my skin.

**

Running is two sports bras, layered
over circulation, each step a gravity punch.
I become a swimmer. We dress & undress
in paper-thin skins. I learn
a thousand ways to be unseen.

**

The first doctor writes *pendular* in my file, tells
me with his face that I am vain & petty. I barely
dress before he shows me the door. A hundred
pounds later, a specialist traces the divots burrowing
into my shoulders, the red branding
circumscribing my ribs, tells me I
should have done this years ago.

**

In two days, I'm making
love, surgical tape still
in place. I have never
felt so beautiful, never
so easy to move. I sleep
shirtless. I always sleep
shirtless.

**

I want to talk about breasts. I am reduced! I am
lifted! Hallelujah & Amen. I know a woman
who has left her breasts behind. I want
to tell her—*I read that article you wrote—it meant
so much to me*—Why
does she look away?

**

Women never say to me, *you really shouldn't
have*. They ask about nursing or pain
even some about identity, if they ask
anything at all. The men though, it's always:
I wish you hadn't. What about me?

**

What about her, my little love? I can feed her,
barely. My arms shake from holding her
up, my nipples are eroding & the milk is only
two ounces, ever. She is so hungry, so tired. I am
the one who did this.

**

Here's something few people know: I
would have chosen a mastectomy, were I
braver. Might have transitioned this body, had I
known that was a choice. Might not
have done it at all, if I had believed
I'd allow myself a daughter.

**

My baby inventories bodies: *Eyes. Toes.
Ears. Nose. Hair. Bellybutton.* Lifts her
shirt &— *Boobs!* she reaches across
to help me find mine, just in case
I missed them.

**

& she tucks her palms between my breasts
snuggles down to sleep, folds herself into
me. Nursing, we'd allow this. But for her,
my weaned one, who allows her
this skin?

**

I have grown into these two
decades' gravity. I love these
faded key-hole scars, soft shelf
bras and my body's simple refusal
to keep shape.

**

At the day spa, a woman with large,
heavy & pendular breasts sits
near me. Her body is
what mine was almost. Still
is. We don't speak. I am
grateful, find her
beautiful.

Gutting the Deer | Cicada Musselman

It is hanging
upside down in the barn.

Someone is going out
to peel its skin off later
with their bare hands.

I have skin too—
holding all this dizzy in.

My own skull is reflected
in my blank eyelids,
wearing flowers of blood.

My stomach wishes for empty.
Empty is clean.
The deer's stomach is full
of dried grass and tree bark,
but we both fattened up in the fall
on the same apples and kale.

I, too, must have this firm liver,
this heart that is just as complex a muscle.
I must remember that
I, too, have this temple for a rib cage.

Twenty Seconds or Death | Rob Geisen

Twenty, as in Matchbox Seconds, as in something people used to run towards at The County Buffet Death, as in that thing over there that threatens to extinguish us into oblivion's old bucket for the entire duration of what's left of anything if we get lazy or relax diligence and don't wash our hands, because people,

these are plague days again and if you hope to stand any goddamn chance of staying alive you've gotta wash your hands 20 seconds each stretch, many, many, many stretches per day after day, after day throughout all of these currently perceivable

treadmills of time and every trip to the sink sinks me to the bottom of this ocean where my base camp was born, where I stand hunched over hand-wrestling myself until the bubbles obliterate counting along with my own mortality each trip to the sink a hoarded reminder of the inevitable, and that every scrubbing at best can only postpone things like *The End*

 Without going into details, and then going into some anyway, I've been freaked out about this whole death thing since I was 5 years old, I don't remember who told me or how I found out but almost immediately after receiving this information I set about trying really hard to flunk kindergarten because being the math genius that I'd been I had it figured out, it was all about numbers, avoiding the numbered grades

Once a kid hit first grade the next thing they'd know, they were in the 2nd and then the following summer would disappear, and they'd be in the 3rd, the numbers methodically escalating on and on like that until before they knew it, they were in the twelfth grade and it was over instead of a gold watch they got a diploma and then they had to get jobs so they got jobs and obvious even to my 5 year old brain back then getting a job inevitably led to death

(I wash, my hands)

and once I'd figured this out, naturally I set about trying really hard to flunk kindergarten

The next day in class I started coloring outside the lines like a fucking lunatic figuring there's no way they can pass me through to the numbered grades if I spectacularly fuck up something as simple as coloring a giraffe

(I wash my hands)

I used every color in the goddamn box that I knew a giraffe not to be and let my arms flail like a manic coyote from my favorite Saturday morning cartoon

(We wash our hands)

and when I was finished with that giraffe it looked like a goddamn nightmare and I smiled to my 5-year-old self-confidence that I'd just side-stepped my own tombstone, but when the teacher came around to check out what I'd done, she just grinned and said something like *That's great, Robbie,* she snatched it off my desk and announced to the class something about what I beautiful job I'd just done while taping the butchered thing to one of the walls

(I wash my hands)

Are you insane?! I screamed in my head, Giraffes don't have purple feet! Obviously, I'm not qualified to continue with this school thing! Why the hell aren't you kicking me out?! I had no idea back then that the system was rigged that fall I was placed in the numbered grades, the grades that went to school all day instead of half, the numbered grades that set off the long countdown to non-existence and doom

(I wash my hands)

and every time I wash my hands I'm reminded of death and I begin shaking again like a neurotically colored giraffe six-ish weeks in and this pandemic has sent my beard rocketing towards the color white

(I wash my hands)

Alive in a fucking pandemic, in bodies that break, I wash my hands and in order to manage the panic I take a look around the apartment: Man-Thing and Kurt Vonnegut resting in completely opposite states of sweater-wearing, against a cold cinder block wall, The Creature From The Black Lagoon romantically stalking a postcard of The Cascades in Michigan

(I wash my hands)

My Grandpa's old binoculars which I've devoted somewhat recently to moon watching

(I wash my hands)

Commodus thumb's downing a King Kong glass The
Kool-Aid Man represents the impossible struggle to
produce an uplifting attitude when you've got ice cubes
floating in the top of your head In order to feel something
in this world other than artificially flavored he has to
throw himself through a fucking wall while trying like hell
not to spill his drink because, literally, he's the drink

(I wash my hands)

I'm tired of washing my hands but the alternative is
horrifying, I wash my hands because as horrible as things
are or potentially can be I'll take the burden of sentience
and the terrifying reminder of impending doom that
washing my hands comes with over flat out non-existence
right now every day in order to manage the panic I've got
the TV running

with the sound off or on, it must be International Mummy
Day, the History Channel's playing the Brendon Frasier
Mummy movies out of order and there's a Bigfoot tele-
series in which almost an entire episode seems devoted to
the hypothesis that maybe Bigfoot doesn't poop which
would make him a true survivor especially during the
earlier weeks of this apocalypse when toilet paper was
harder to spot than Bigfoot

(I wash my hands)

Fuck you, commercial, with your pandering assertions that
Burger King loves me and unwanted premonitions of
alternate possibilities and life-threatening genital
infections (yeast)

Al Pacino laughing at Keanu Reeves while getting his dick sucked in The Devil's Advocate, that's how I feel as an American every time Trump's on TV giving another one of his live Trump commercial-slash-coronavirus updates

Not the Al Pacino

(I wash my hands)

I feel like the Keanu Reeves

Love Poem from an Avocado | Lee Frankel Goldwater

My seed slides out easily, only for you,
As you bite into my green, silky pulp.
Though I am wrinkled and a little bit soft,
I know you will still, always love me.
As you mix me with spice and dip your best into me,
Sinking your teeth in, ravenously, consuming every bit,
Making my body part of your own.
And even though I'm great at parties,
I prefer it when you keep me all to yourself,
And I'm pretty sure,
You do too.

Quarantine Dinner | Liza Katz Duncan

Outside the open window above the stove, weeds and a
pile of bricks. The vines covering the back fence didn't
flower this year. Sunday and the children should be
crowding the playgrounds; the churches should be letting
out; the baby should be six weeks old.

A barbecue punctures the evening. Smell of sap and
s'mores, snap of kindling. Someone shouts Alexa, play
Brown Eyed Girl. I can't pinpoint when we started to
worry about leaving the house, or stopped going out for
groceries. It must have been around the first of spring,

the baby's birthday. Here in the quiet kitchen,
I've been staring out the window too long. I've
burned the last of the pantry staples again,
canned beans and frozen vegetables unsalvageable,
permeated with smoke, charred garlic. I scrape the
evidence into the trash, leave the saucepan to soak.

The smoke alarm shakes you from your sleep under two
afghans, in the television's halo. You emerge from the
living room shirtless, with matted hair. Dinner, a
makeshift salad and rice, stale bread to sop up the
dressing. There's not much to say: in two months neither
of us has spoken to anyone else in person.

When we're done eating, you say,
Don't clear the table. Don't get up. I got
it, you say, as if,

if I move, the dishes will clatter to the
floor. Who knows what else might
come apart in my clumsy hands.

The Four-Year Itch | Hannah Skewes

It itches,
the back of my hand
with its new topology:
rivers of soap and raised beds
of dead skin cells,
monsoon fear
I can't scratch away
no matter how satisfying
it would be
if I could.

I am infected with
notions
that most of us
know better,
drowning in almost summertime
and I can't breathe through the cotton.

It's the blank faces
that give me nightmares,
the ones who still own
Alamo Placita grass
and center sidewalk privilege.

I know it means something
to suffocate ourselves,
all together now,
and I am listening, I am *listening,*

and I am itching, my hands are
itching
to hold onto something
without smearing it all
with blood.

Quotidian Delivery | Kierstin Bridger

You mail trinkets and ephemera
useful mysteries to puzzle out.
I made a paper boat
from the tissue you sent.
The violet petals
were my first passengers
in the same flower envoy
you shot through the air
enveloped in the soft
craft brown of your missive.

That is how it is with all we take home:
a day's worth of pocket change,
the missile of news
exploding across the airwaves,
my daughter returning for dinner,
Swedish fish on her breath.
We suss, we suss.

Did you know we often text each other here—
quiet in opposing rooms of the same house?
We used to yell in mine. We could hide
slip out a door. . .
I know almost nothing of how you grew up.

Sorting through the day
I find memories flood in.
I tell myself to bail, set a new course
like any good captain loyal to her ship.
Reroute, reroute
I whisper, adjust the sail.

Sometimes I picture you and your shore,
your choppy wind
and unexpected cloud cover
so many miles away from where I stand.

In Other News | Eric Raanan Fischman

Jupiter slings asteroids at the Earth
like Cupid's arrows. Planets make love
by colliding. A star falling around
a black hole paints a lovely rosette.
Before the Chicxulub impact, dinosaurs
were great swimmers. Scientists have
brought back to life an extinct shade
of blue. The longest living thing is a
150 foot string that hunts in spirals.
Those colored lights in the sky were
never military test planes, the US
government confirms. The biggest
hole in the ozone layer has been healed.
The coronavirus has been translated
into music. Archaeologists have unearthed
the world's oldest piece of string. High
speed gas collisions in galaxies are
the most effective contraception for stars.
Quantum computing is easy. Algae
can gallop. Peacock spiders can dance.
90 million years ago the South Pole
was a rainforest, and it can be again.
Einstein was right. About everything.

Ode to the Avocado | Tricia Knoll

Oh, if I wanted
one perfect roundness to fit
my hand as sweetly as an egg,
it's you, avocado.

Lob your dark green skin north
for salsa and fresh-squeezed limes.
Soothe my tongue ravaged
by sharp-toothed words,
conform to my teeth,
invite my tongue to roll in bland
oil of green.

Teach me timing.
You are as unforgiving about being ignored
in the juniper bowl as the banana.
You rot inside out, mellow green to black
like jealousy.

The places that know you best
– La Fonda in Sante Fe –
guarantee perfection, guacamole
brought to the table every night,
mashed with garlic, jalapenos,
tomato, onion, sea salt, and lime.

Open up. I love your womb,
pregnant curves shielding
your nut-hard seed that yields
last to the worm's work.

Like women,
you've been squeezed
in markets from Maine
to Mazatlan.
There is no other way
to know how ripe you are.

First published on VisitantLit

All Am I, I Am All | Robert Beveridge

The potatoes never taste
the way they did in your
grandmother's, no matter
how you prep them. Today's
experiment: pepper, cumin,
two drops of blood from as
close to the heart as possible.

The crucible reaches critical
mass, and in they go with two
jalapeños and a handful
of cattails marinated in neon.
All you can do now is stir,
stir, stir until it smells just
right or the top of your head
comes off, whichever is first.

Roses Encased in Glass: We Were Too Eager, The Little Prince Knew This | Gwendalynn Roebke

I have been keeping a garden
In small terracotta pots.

There I've let my heart grow again
From seed.

Overambitious, the basil
Chokes one another,
Bends over and dies.

I must practice
Reaching for sunlight and sipping water,
Press lips to leaves,
Play melancholy ballads,
In seven different languages.

I want sustenance in sorrow
Spanning across the globe,
Croon to them in only 2 tongues,
Let them know my voice,
My heart, I'll tend to you twice a day,
Tell you stories of rotten roots,
Of the others buried behind my memories,
Insufferable heat, sweating in subzero temperatures.

I will watch you,
Moon flower and lemon balm,
Break the soil.

I've waited too long for my own reunion.

I am the invasive knotweed | Caroline Savery

I am the invasive knotweed.

I am indigenous to Earth.

I infiltrate all territories.

My adaptability is my survival tactic.

I dominate a degraded landscape.

Like lichen   like silt
I layer and stick,   I drift,
like a pollen node I float on the breeze.

I'll make anywhere my home.

Denied access privileges
    for my ragged hew,
    my breeding stock,
    my unsightly view,
owning all with a simple, direct,
humility.

I hear all.

I will listen.

I fear not your struggle,
and will help walk you through it

for I *understand*.

My one power—to understand
is the skeleton key
that yields forbidden treasures unto me.

I love my life, and know
this is authority enough.

I spread myself,
I ramble lush.

These spade-shaped alternating leaves
till your turf
I so will contain all
in my one shape.

Mutability is kindness.
Adaptability is (intelligence
Equanimity is) wisdom.

Note: Japanese knotweed is a rugged, hardy, tall-growing, decadent-looking invasive found all over Pittsburgh, PA, where I lived for circa 8 years. However, like dandelion, Japanese knotweed is edible (if you take the time to prepare it!)

Isolation is My Destiny | Syed Aamir Sharief Qadri

People of the world,
listen to me with all ears.

I am Kashmir,
the land of isolation.

Today you cry of being singled out
inside homes you thump your head.

Is it that you lost all your hope
for a few days of constraint?

Look at me,
just look at me.

I am sequestered for three decades;
max times my people are coerced
to reside inside their homes.

Don't mislay hope,
look at me.

Learn from me how to kill time.

Today I offer you help.

You may or may not be with me
but I am and will always be with you.

My pledge is not to let you feel low.

I will stimulate your energy
with my sagas of seclusion.

Corona will go away and
very soon you will have liberty
free from segregation
free from aggravation.

But after Corona,
new quirks will come my way
and impel me again to survive at home
because Isolation is my destiny.

DYING FREE | mayryanna

Children of the mountain
Blood of the deer and fox
running deeper than our father's
Blind to the actualities
fenced into paranoia
They were afraid of our freedom
So we ran ourselves
all through the forests
We tasted the ancient Truth fully
We listened to the wisdom
far too real to be heard

It entered through our souls feeling
Life like this is treasure
something better than gold
Silver dimmer than these wild fancies
Perhaps it's too expensive
costing our very lives
Our tainted mountain blood flowing
One, two, three, more...
So many young, dead
Yet somehow, they never leave these fields
Still racing around the mountains
Still hunting the caves of predators
Still collecting treasure: bones and feathers
Their spirits dance on the wind
Voices whispering in the silence
Forever safe, held by branches of the forest
We do not cry for these children
They know love greater than we
They lived fast on the mountain, dying free

Some day we will join them
Once again we'll play together
in our mountain kingdom thriving, wildly

Tomatoes | Mary Christine Delea

Unlike mysterious apricots and lemons,
the histories of which hover out of our grasp,
we know you, fruit of an empire, staple of the Aztecs.
You grew to 15,000 types in all colors, growing

wild throughout the Andes.

You spread worldwide even after
you were tamed into gardens
grown by novices and experts alike.

Shaped like a heart, you entranced
Thomas Jefferson,
conquered Roman reserve
to create generations of romantics making marinara.
Recipes passed down for pomodori ripieni,

goulash, panzaella, mousaka, goloubki, tabouli,

gazpacho, menemen, pa amb tomaquet, borscht,
tiki masala, adobo, curry, shakshuka.

No culture untouched, you were unstoppable.

But supermarkets.
But shipping.
But fast food and plastic containers.
Your numbers were choked down to the largest,
reddest, most consistent;

your unique varieties, the oddly shaped,

those feral flavors went
largely forgotten, became extinct.
All those gardeners spend

summers cursing

your numbers on their vines,
giving you away to city friends,
slicing you into sandwiches, chopping you into
salads featuring every other fruit and vegetable,
creaming you for

soups,

and creating sauces and salsas
until there is no more room
for another Mason jar in the pantry

or Tupperware tub in the freezer.

Then they curse you more. You persevere,
but with little of the dignity that was once yours
when Xipe Totec was prayed to for your growth
and people welcomed your abundance.

Live is a Strange Word | Grace Mitchell

This morning I couldn't tell
if you were home,
so I acted as though you were not
Closing doors without thought
of the soft click the door made,
walking about the kitchen,
not shifting my feet to avoid
the various creaks in that old, warped wood

I even left the house several times—
but not because I was afraid of you

And in a week you will not
live here anymore—
although "live" is a strange word
for whatever it is you do—

Soon I will be free of you,
(only in truth I was
free of you the moment
I started pretending you were gone,
and in truth I will not
be free of you
until I stop dreading the ways
in which I take up space).

Your Handwriting | Steven Sassman

the Poetry leapt from her breast

crushed through her pen
and lit the page
on fire

she'd been taught
to dress it up
in pretty paper rhymes

but the Poetry was too big
to fit

she tried and tried
to wrestle it into a poem
but the Poetry blazed through
the useless lines
jumped from
the burning page
broke out
her window
seared a path across
the neighborhood
and town

set the hills
on fire

and streaked up high
into the air

The sky wasn't big enough

the Poetry eclipsed
the sun

all the poets turned away their faces
bitter with jealousy

but the flash hung in their eyes
and haunted their hearts

and all the shock waves
alerted the army
men came
and took her from her home

the Americans tortured her
Insisting

we know this is your handwriting

but all she could do was scream

it wasn't me

it wasn't me

it wasn't me

A.T. | John Staughton

After This,
perhaps I'll take a dozen lovers
or just hold a hundred hands so well
we fall asleep satisfied
and call back before lunch,
and on those hundred second dates
we'll play footsie
and forget what we ordered
because we forgot how to order,
but not how to fall

Dear checkout girl,
after this I will see your smile
and return it
tenfold over my billfold—
I miss lipstick and smirks,
tangled beards and double-chins,
dainty noses burst from
blossom cheeks.

After this, fellow stranger,
I won't turn from your eyes
cross the train,
nor drop mine to distraction,
or ignore a dusky howl

>   because after this we'll remember
>   the hibernation Nature scripted
>   the turn of day to
>   night
>   when sacred things occur

                              prayers offered
                                   spells cast
                        chanting on fresh earth
                           in lieu of dawn's return

After this,
I want to rub elbows again,
and get bumped in the street—
you apologize
and then I do
and we laugh,
pausing close
enough to smell your perfume,
and know if you had
peanut butter for breakfast.

I want to kiss you again
and carbon-date the
smoke in your hair,
so I know how long it's been
since your last campfire.
I want to taste the sweat
on your secret-keeping skin,
flushing finally
desperate for touch,
for laughter to knock our knees
in the dark, to scrub
bad memories from my tongue
and tumble dry in strong, strange arms.

            Remember dates and destinations,
                when hugs weren't taboo,

                and porn was more than venue nostalgia?

After this,
I will befriend the next soul
beside me on a plane,
and learn their family secrets
why they travel
deep opinions
on the in-flight meal—
I will want every detail,
of your simply shining life
unfilled by headphones
or elsewhere fantasy.

                We will remember that being close
                      has always been precious

I want to deliver packages
and shake hands
I want to schmooze on stoops
riff on rooftops,
I won't even mind your smalltalk
just give me
a clap on the back
the crow's feet of a stranger
a smoke-filled dancehall
and your moves
and your pulse
beside mine
for a night
or ten

After this
I will stretch out
to ask for a squeeze,
or a concert in the park
for your knee under the table
your head under my skirts
for you to be the big spoon
one more time,
last time, I promise,
but when you grab my hand,
you'll find my fingers crossed.

Scream | Veronica Love

Scream

Let it rise in your throat

And you throw your head back to release the sound

Scream

As your voice cracks
And your throat struggles to meet the need
rolling up your esophagus
rattling your uvula

Scream

rumbling from your guts
escaping from your cells
Boiling up and tearing tissue

Scream

With rage
With passion
With anger
With sorrow

With pain
With necessity

Scream

Release
Freedom
Hope

Scream

Pull back together what you can
And try again tomorrow

You are not meditating | Agnes Vojta

You are not meditating
You're not reading
the classics.
not practicing
barre cords on the guitar,
not brushing up
on your French.
You're just hanging on,
for dear life
by your fingernails.
You're trying.
Trying
not to eat too much chocolate,
not to snap at your kids,
not to drink too much,
not to cry when you think of
what you're missing,
and whom.
You are doing
the best you can.
You shower. You work.
You cook, you eat.
You sleep, badly,
and get up in the morning
and do it all over again.
Sometimes, you walk outside
and are astonished
that it is spring.
Sometimes, you breathe
a little deeper
and imagine a life

after this.
Sometimes you stop
beating yourself up
for not doing quarantine
the right way.

Good vs. Typical | Connor Orrico

on good days it is amorphous

energizing sport bodywash,

mint zing toothpaste and corporate

abstractions like phoenix

or black eclipse deodorant

underneath hand cream

with a faint bouquet of

peach and all its purity

on a more typical day

it is the humbler scent

of stale unwashed sheets,

sharp saccharine breath

from energy drinks and

individually wrapped candies,

a transient veneer to mask

the musty smell of being human

Blue Boy | Kristin LaFollette

And when you became the youngest,
       you earned blood & the first thing
       we saw was blood —

You were a paper mâché animal and
       I rinsed the pulp from your body,
           cracked you open and explored
           what was inside,

found twigs and sticks turned to powder,
              little bruises pink with scar tissue
       and
    soft fiber,

the price of being born reckless
with so much blood pouring
           down your back —

I had to create space for you in my mind,
       new soil for our shared history and root,

                   had to find delicate hands so
         that
            I could touch your
transparent skin —

1996,

that's when the trouble started —

At first, I counted your bones

and wondered how you could
come from such cold and snow

                but *you moved* &
                        you moved &

I didn't know then:
       How attached I would become,
           How I would make you into
           the same kind of winged
           bird as me,

How you were never meant to be kept,
your December body both
                      hunter & arrow—

Mother's Day Conversations vs Those at Teas with Mabel | Nicole Taylor

As she walks into the kitchen
with cooked steak from her son,
septuagenarian Helen, Pete's mom,
tells me, *I still have your dance*
advertising boards.
She already told me this, and my teacher.

I want you to cut my ivy and
you can write about it, she tells me.
Weeks later I widely prune
for four hours English Ivy
that is killing several Douglas Firs in the yard.
I also prune some wild invasive cucumber plant
and soda cans.

Our older tired sister Angela and our septuagenarian mom
sit in the front room, drink chardonnay, and discuss their work.

We listen to Smith House politics.
My older sister tells us of her desire to assist
on the presidential campaign.
I want to do paperwork.
If anyone objects to my opinions while canvassing, I'd blow up.

Really! says Pete sarcastically.
Later there is little debate
over salad preferences.
Tom will not eat tomatoes.

This is shared every holiday.

Unlike teas with Mabel.
Acceptable. Agreeable.

My friendly apartment neighbor Mabel
accepts
her sons
not talking
to each other
and then she
accepts me
to tea and conversation.

She offers
apple cinnamon,
lemon zest,
orange, or
raspberry tea
She doesn't
drink alcohol
like her parents did not.
Acceptable.

Mabel places
Snickerdoodles,
sugar cookies
or carrot,
zucchini or
pumpkin bread
on a plate or saucer.
Mabel tells me about her
sons visiting from Seattle and Sacramento.

Agreeable.

Mabel says about
low-income living, housing and healthcare applications.
In her mid-eighties, her health seems fair
and she's got few complaints or quibbles in her life.
We agree to watch or listen to public broadcasting with
her.

Jeff Bezos | Brice Maiurro

Jeff Bezos has never idled in his car
in queue for a fast food drive-thru
screaming up from the banshee
smoke of a 96' junker clunker.

Jeff Bezos hasn't thrown his phone into a public
swimming pool and watched as his March TGI Friday's
paycheck dissolves into the black hole ether of a regretful
Tuesday night where up above the lifeguard station is
empty and there is no one there to save you.

Jeff Bezos hasn't magicked soup
up from the dirty ground, dug his
fire element hands into the morbid
earth and pulled up blood red turnips
from their screaming limbs to pluck
their fragile roots, sending them from
one life to be reborn into the acidic pit
of an empty belly.

He hasn't sung in traffic in December
in snow almost late
to something. He's always departing
and never arriving. He becomes a tree
in the shadow of a skeleton highrise
under the eerie loom of streetlight negligence,
each evening starving a little more
for the true nutrients of the sun
he has forgotten.

Jeff Bezos plays tapes
on how to cry in private.

The sound pours in
through every perfect speaker
in his house but there is no music.

He is orbited by disoriented mirrors.
Desperate to look them in his eyes.
They look and he does not look back.

Jeff Bezos wakes to find he has no face;
an unpainted portrait like an undaunted
digital canvas expectant of code that
commands but is never in conversation.

Jeff Bezos is beneath the world
on the summit of a mountain.

He runs with wings made of fire.

He pretends to sleep in a temporary room
to a neverending knock on his doornail.

He opens his door expectant of flowers
and is met by the mask of red death.

He offers the flowers that line his room
but the hands of the mask are spoken for
carrying an absent gift,

delivered in time that he does not own.

Signed up for a 365 Day Amazon Prime Subscription, but didn't expect to get- | Maggie Saunders

    Live Streaming of-

        Luxury Amidst Chaos

        Unsustainable Survivor

        New Age Doomsday Preppers

    Delivery Now of novel pathogens

    Repeat delivery of history

    Free global shipping.

There's a Particular Way my Mother Cooks | Erica Hoffmeister

Her hips dance around sharp edges of the rough-cut tile
counters in the track home she rents, so unlike the home we
owned once—dressed in hand-laid brick at the bottom of a
vast hill of jagged rock—so very much the same

She likes to toss in ingredients as she goes:
dash of this
handful of that

I assume this is the epitome of woman
I grow to learn this is how you make a home:
home - maker

When our house at the bottom of the hill burned down, the
kitchen remained. The hearth of each of us eight children—
stones laid, then removed as we moved
out, and on

> [Once, I used a chisel to remove the flooring from my bedroom—on hands and knees, I chipped each morsel of adhesive from concrete, scraped evidence of the past into crumbs I brushed into a dustpan and discarded, laboriously sanded grooves and scars and wrinkles smooth, then painted the entire floor a glossy black.
>
> My mother did not react, did not mention longevity or finite decisions I often made in passing destruction disguised as *fresh starts*.]

broke her heart with each meal emptier
than the last. She never could learn how to cook for less
than a mob

When I was twenty-six years old, I lived alone and learned—

> [This should not be a shock or surprise to anyone in modern times, but for me, four months of solitude was a goddamn record. My whole life I had roomed with a baker's dozen children, too many parents, and dogs, cats, cousins, and friends, crashing roommates that would overstay others' definitions of welcome—though for us, this measurement was boundless.
>
> To prove familial dedication, or: to test the limits of her boundaryless love, my mother and I shared her room the year before I turned 30, when I needed the warmth of her electric fireplace, comfort of her small balcony that offered a dirt-field view beyond a California-privacy fence, the chlorine-smell of neighbors' pools, convenience of a walk-in closet and adult-sized tub, a fresh-cooked meal each evening before her shifts. I smeared self over each and every swath of drywall and Spanish tile. Let's face facts: I have always been a terrible roommate.]

I am a beautiful cook. In my lonesome kitchen filled with colonial eastern sunlight, a harmony of existence from within those big, bay windows, I cooked myself meals as if they were feasts. I imagined my mother as I tested recipes from scratch, collected cookbooks from basements and yard-sales, fingered hand-written marginal notes and deciphered memories of movement—taught myself how to cook on my own with her reckless fistfuls of spice and sage.

Often, my mother's dishes did not come out. The all-berry pie was always soupy, garlic accidentally swapped for salt. Re-creation of meals was near-impossible—we silently savored the dishes we loved, knowing full well we may never taste the creation of those flavors and textures in our mouths within those fleeting moments ever again. In truth, it's a wonder anything was edible with the way she refused to record recipes, or even follow ones that were written. Cooking,
she'd say, is like travel—

> What good is a map, if your head is buried
> in it? What kinds of lives are baked as precisely
> as bread?

It's the notes between the margins that matter:
> *a little pasta water in the sauce*
> *a pinch of sugar in the pizza dough*
> *some garlic powder sprinkled on top*
> *10 or 15 or 25 minutes should do it, just check every so often*

Hock Messer* | Wendy Mannis Scher

Alaska natives name the blade *ulu*,
but I know the tool by another handle—
red enamel riveted to stainless steel
fisted in the shallow curve of an oak bowl.
Nana worked in pale cotton, a house
dress, iron smooth, billowing floral against
flecked formica. She minced roasted livers,
onions, hard-boiled eggs laced with schmaltz.
Every spring in her hot apartment, we gathered:
Nana, Aunties, Mama, me hammering
the keen edge of memory against each other's
stories, slicing meaning until nothing
remained but silence, and the thick brown paste
we smeared on matzoh—the taste of mettle.

Yiddish for mezzaluna chopping knife.

Día de los Muertos | Ken Farrell

The road home was long
and a long time—ten years—
since my mother
had run away with my father
who smirked and said
she was beautiful
with a little Irish in her.
She nuzzled his neck
murmured over and over
my man of valor, my man of valor.

Wildflowers late-
bloomed along Texas right-
of-ways, some of them just
alive, sepals and petals
curled like palsied hands,
most of them already dead
along the edge of mother's childhood
home, scattered
along sidewalks and streets
and I knew: Trinidad
was different.

My grandmother sweated
over the steaming cauldron
of Candelaria, my grandfather
saw-dusted from his work,
the many slip-shod half-sized
caskets leaned on walls
scattered like macabre dice
around their yard.

Both of them smiled, spoke
at once in rapid Spanish—
I couldn't understand
yet my mother answered quickly—
and they looked with tilted heads
at my Irish father and backpedaled
through the coffins
with wide arm gestures
welcomed us into the house.

My grandfather looked down
big brown eyes
reached out
a callused brown hand
patted my head
his accent as thick as his grin
and said: *You ready for Halloween?*
I nodded.
What you gonna be? Un esqueleto?
he asked. My blue eyes
teared. Daunted by the brawny
silence, I said finally
Wonderwoman, unsure.   *Wonderwoman.*

The Invisible Indispensable | Galen Bernard

A chef wrote in the *NYT* that she's not sure
if her restaurant will have reason to exist after this.
If her work will be wanted
if her place will have a place...

and I wished to send her a tonic
brewed of my memories.

The clank and clamor of forks on plates.
The sizzle and scent of flesh in pans.

The dance of seating that charted a romance.

Across the table for firsts.
On to adjacent when familiar.
Until the tender triumph of sliding around to the same side.

I miss the discovery of the previously unknown delight.
The return to an early comfort found in a familiar dish.

The looks between bites.
The laughs spluttered during sips.

Each of my closest relationships
can tie its bond to a restaurant or bar.

Back all the way
to four teen boys at the buffet,
putting pepper in the cup of whoever went to refill a plate.

Forward to a man and a woman,
fresh into their thirties,
feeling out whether if they let their lives fill with indulgence
it would be met with the same care
as the saké in front of them,
flowing over the edges of each glass
into a wooden box below.

Eating at a restaurant is the first thing I want to do
when this dissonance of distance ends.
Well, the first thing in public.

I realize this won't end.
That there is no going back to before.
Only a continuing, an evolving.

But if I could go back,
Back to normal, back to nascent, back to just a moment prior to now,
I would return to a restaurant.

Instead, I return to a bookmark I bought
At a market after a meal in Spain.
When that was a sentence you could say.

"Lo esencial es invisible para los ojos" it reads.
What is essential is invisible to the eye.

Moussaka | Janette Schafer

Leathery skin of eggplant loosens,
flesh softens in the roasting pan.
Sliced sweet potatoes, tender,
yield to the fork. He wipes a blob

of creamy melted béchamel from his
mother's face. The lentils shuck
their coats, onions brown in their bath
of butter and olive oil.

Her false teeth fall on her lower lip.
He sets her spoon on the tablecloth,
resets her teeth in their right place.

Hunger Map | Anna White

Fifty small feet across
the long backyard,
over the metal fence,
veering to the right,
up the old tree and there
you could sit, peeling
back the thin branches' bark
expose the dry, white flesh-
> best eaten on hot afternoons
> with hours to go before dinner.

Out the front door
down the tall wooden steps
quick bare feet over the hot street
into the open lot and
through the thin trees,
you could dig deep with little fingers
to unearth another specialty:
wild and spicy spring onion-
> best eaten raw while
> sheltered in the shade.

Now, head west to the public park
throw yourself down
centered in the grassy field
and with patience and precision
gently pull the blades of grass
to reveal that classic childhood delicacy:
those tender roots—
best eaten upside down
under blue sky.

Three long city blocks to the east,
left down the alley,
half-way up on the right side,
a true treasure: blackberry bush on public ground—
> best eaten in bare feet
> after three o'clock rain.

Two full blocks to the west,
right smack on the communal corner:
crab apples,
loads of them,
stuffed into pockets and shirts and mouths—
> best eaten with one's older brothers
> with a better reach.

Now, thirty years down this meandering path,
countless turns left and right,
east and west, north and south,
and circles, so many circles,
but in a sudden open valley today,
memories of scarcity and hunger
coming to me more mildly
as a picture of abundance.

The Best Way to Eat a Grape | Deborah Edler Brown

The best way to eat a grape is when your
mother peels it for you. It must be
green and oval. She pokes into the
endskin with her nail. She cups it in one
hand and takes back the skin a strip at a
time. Sometimes she casts it aside.
Sometimes she eats it. But she hands you
an egg of naked pulp and into your
mouth it goes, sweet, pure flesh of
fruit. The best way to eat a grape is
stripped naked by your mother and offered
one at a time. She peels, you eat. And
you don't have to be five.

The Kitchen is the Soul of the Family | Morgan L. Ventura

The caskets always face upward toward the sky
perhaps to facilitate a floating soul.

The heart's no longer a flickering ember
or thumping clump of magma from
Mount Vesuvius' sputtering, frenzied mouth.
After dinner they serve us coffee,

pizzelles, and biscotti, so dry that I spit them out
to the sound of laughter: "What kind
of Italian likes moist cookies?
They're only as good as the coffee you dip them in."

Death brings family together
but then cleaves them apart
with the heaviest knife.

Malocchio visits, and then visits again,
in a garlic-laden kitchen sprinkled with Sicilian
words and fragrances.
"Do not answer the door, instead throw salt."

The golden horn that graced my grandfather's olive skin
wards off ill-intentioned, jealous *Malocchio*, the Evil Eye.
Golden hunchback swaying from his same necklace chain
reminds me:
"Be good to those who have drawn the lesser lot in this
world."

The kitchen is the soul of the family,
no one is complete without the art of cookery.

Memories are bubbles bursting tomatoes,
popping from the chanting of clams
and golden garlic; plates of cured meats sing of lemons,
bergamot, and n'duja.

Death brings family together
but then cleaves them apart
with the heaviest knife.

I do not want to eat in fake Italian restaurants
for the rest of my life. I am sorry
I did not learn more. Sifting through tattered boxes,
I find a note on yellowed paper
worn thin with the passing of time,
translucent and luminous.
My Great Nonna wrote:

"I hear you are a beautiful child. Your grandfather tells me this,
and he never says anything is beautiful unless it truly is."
Reading graceful, spiraling letters, I ingest the planetary
predictions my Sicilian ancestor traced through the stars,

a cosmology of love and light, a life
mapping vibrant corridors of this world and what's to come.
This identity, so rejected,
returns with raging vengeance,

an intensity of a thousand glass doors shattered rather than
opened by way of mourning. When the casket is brought out,
when I see his spirit pass through the doors to the parlor,
wandering, lost, echoing in staccato,

"To have known, to have known."
The worst possible dirge.

Pizzelles on the table, coffee growing stale,
as those familiar and strange show up to pay respects.
I'm haunted by these dry, powdered stars
from the funerary spread that augur grief.

Death brings family together but then cleaves me apart.

Some Afternoon | Riley Welch

At this point in isolation,
I have listened to all the albums I have ever loved,
eaten all the food my stomach can handle,
and even still, with so little to do,
I burn the potatoes in the oven.

Christmas Cookies | David-Matthew Barnes

His mother kisses my cheek, leaves behind just a smudge
of crimson. I feel the comfort of her green silk dress and I
know why he is so calm. I cling to

the tray of cookies she baked just for me, balancing them
on the tip of my heart and the edge of my smile - it never
falters, not even when the snow is heavy.

She bundles up in her wool scarf and gloves,
her knitted hat. I watch her fingers tremble over each
black button of her tattered winter coat. But it's her
memories that keep her

warm. Back to Little Italy she goes to meet her Sicilian
friends. Amongst candles, Mass and spirit, she will
explain why her son has no bride. Crumbs will fill my lap.

Maybe next year, I will get a sweater.

Two Poems | Mary Anna Kruch

For My Father, Gidio

I stand at the door
of your childhood home
and I think to myself,
we draw breath from the same sky.

I seek brown eyes—my eyes—
and arms that draw me in,
offer ageless affection;
I ache for insight
of the abyss that grows
when children leave
and parenti* perish;
I crave broad, Roman faces,
twinkling recognition,
voices that croon
dialect,
a sky that enfolds the house
that still holds you and welcomes me.

The door has been removed,
the concrete and stone structure
is wide open,
but it is full.

Ancient farm implements rest
where you once did.

Back then, did you look up
into the same night sky,
count the same stars, dream of America –
as I dream of returning to this same spot?

The newer house is concrete,
two floors rather than one, tiled, not dirt.

You could have used all these rooms
for your cousins, who had shared the space.
How many of your father's family
have lived in that house, farmed the land,
worked in the vineyard and olive grove?
Did you help feed and care for the animals?

Vittorio and Pierina build on tradition
as they build onto the house
for a returning son.
They look after the farm,
reduced in size over time – acres sold to survive
droughts and poor harvests, pay bills.
Camilla, Vittorio's mother, has recently died;
all but one child grown, gone,

settled, with families of their own.
The old and new homes stand side by side.
At the inside door to the outdoor kitchen,
plastic strips hang to allow the air to flow,
to welcome the farm dog
and the cat who rides his back.

The stove uses gas not wood;
the storeroom is stocked with farina,
newly-made pasta, salame,
wine lined up on the shelf,

awaiting sustenance and celebration.
An attached dining room
holds a wooden table
beneath a roof of clay tiles.
Even now there is much to celebrate:
births, holidays, saints' days –
visits from American cousins.

Bread cools on the counter;
fresh basil, sautéed garlic, tomatoes
simmer in the day's sauce.
A simple *insalada mista*** has been prepared.
We sit down for la cena,
finding a table simply set;
red wine, salami, and fresh bread
wait, teasing appetites.

Oh, how I wish you were here.

* *parenti* (Italian: relatives)
** *insalada mista* (Italian: mixed salad)

For My Grandfather, Giacinto | Mary Anna Kruch

I return to the farm in Pofi
and stand on a slight rise
overlooking acres of olives, grapes, and fields.
Under an open, cloudless sky,
I squint through the brilliant sun and imagine you,
old straw hat on your head, hoe in your hand.
The air is balmy with the redolence
of freshly-turned earth.
Your brother Vincenzo guides
a horse-drawn harrow a few rows over;
you both started at dawn, feeding the animals,
but you are young and have energy to spare,
even in the afternoon heat.

The same sun that deepened olive brown skin,
as he worked the soil
and pruned the vines a century ago,
glows through me now.
I walk along rows of tomatoes and peppers,
admire the grapes and olives –
bless those rays that hold me, body and soul.
Closing my eyes, I hear the sheep,
a tractor hum;
a soft wind ruffles olive branches
when the work is through.

Returning to the house, you think of dinner,
smell the pasta in red sauce
and crusty bread baked that morning.
You will uncork the wine
that you and Vincenzo made last year,
pour generous glasses for the adults,
small ones for the children.
The work has been hard and the day long,
so you will converse little as you eat.
But as the day cools, you will sit outside with the family,
peel some oranges, handing sections to the children.
Talk with Nonna* Luisa will be light,
as the sky moves to navy blue.

Today, as I turn toward the outdoor kitchen,
I know that homemade pasta in red sauce,
warm bread, and wine await me.
After dinner, my cousins, *la mia famiglia***
will sit beneath the covered veranda, nibbling on fruit,
and I will lean into the language of my family,
contributing little – but understanding much.

* Nonna (Italian: Grandmother)
**la mia famiglia (Italian: my family)

4:36 am | Jacob Ian DeCoursey

Dreams become ghosts.

Forgetting is
a haunted house.

Vague shapes crawl on
the ceiling. My
eyes close, and I

reach to touch your
sleeping body.
Be there. Be there.

A Pandemic Note to Self | Hayden Dansky

You are no savior,
just a piece of the puzzle.
You are no warrior,
but you do fight like hell.
Picked that one up
as a young child with the
dandelions you made your crown from
With the four-leaf clovers from the patch you found
between where the bus dropped you off
and where you stashed your bike in the woods
to get home
held on to it like
no amount of luck
would save you but
the time spent picking could.

Your body is small
and curled up and defeated and shamed.
Your body is huge
if you consider your tongue.
If you climb out of the box she built for you
before you were born,
stand on it instead
grab a mic and lose yourself for a while—
You will always crawl back in
once you speak.
You'll use the backlash of being big
to punish yourself with,
to bring yourself down with
until you stand up and try again.

All you have built
stays steady in the pandemic
while the institutions crumble.
You see why sharing power and
staying close to the grass
is not only about respect, but resiliency.
You remember every day
you laid down in the grass
felt your body on the earth
lost yourself between the
blades and the petals
imagined a new world where
small looked big
all of a sudden—
let your small body become a giant bug, now.

You've spent the last decade as a food rescue organizer,
a food justice advocate,
redistributing produce and power
resources and health
but starving yourself in the name of freedom.
Could you consider for a moment that you deserve to live
in the world you're trying to create?

Some days you scream for a seat at the table,
then shut your door and
muffle your mouth and
hide behind
a stay at home order
when there seems to be no spot for you to speak
in the links you call into.
They say, if you don't get a seat at the table
just pull one up,

as if it were simple
as if it doesn't touch all your core wounds
as if it doesn't remind you of the years you spent
eating on the ground, off the ground
as if you don't have to shake out your trauma
to make sure you can fit into the chair.

You are not the shapeshifter that you think you are—
You are a coyote in a suit.
When you speak,
you only howl.
You see, it's not just that they cannot
see the invisible,
they cannot understand it, too, and
you wonder why the hell you tried
wearing that damn button-up
in the first place.
Just because you travel alone doesn't mean you are—
Your whole team is a highly organized family pack.
You are not alone.
When you listen,
you will remember
that you have never been.

This doesn't mean that the truth
of your efforts are not worth sharing—
When all that we know falls around us,
it's hard to see what's true at first.
If they've never seen the margins
it's hard to notice their power and vibrancy.
If they see black and brown bodies
and don't pay attention to their light.
If they see white bodies

and actually think that is what is pristine and pure,
when their towers collapse
when their rules collapse
when their systems collapse
it will be the poor that offers them bread
it will be the ones they fear that take them in
the ones they criticized they ask for help from.
It will be the queer and weird and trans and disabled and
dark and indigenous
that find what they need.

Those of us who live in the liminal spaces, or are kin to it
It will be those of us who spent our childhood days
laying in the grass searching for luck
to save ourselves with
that know what roots look like
and how to make tea from them.
How to thank them.
How to let go.
Fall into this earth like it's your home.
It's always been.

The ghosts of movement ancestors
will remind you of your place—
That you are not responsible for the end,
but for every step forward instead.
That we all take steps back
That we all fall to the ground
and lay there for a while—
That there are so many more names than we know
that nurtured survival,
turned the soil for it.
Gave their hope

to the compost,
their despair, too.

Compost your despair tonight,
try growing something new.
Let it bud like the crocus and the daffodils
that shine brightly in the spring snow,
although they already know
it's coming again,
but are committed to April magic.

Compost your despair
Your hope
Your stories
Your critique
Your tragedy—
Let the earth swallow you
and hold it all,
This earth that actually wants to
let it turn for just tonight.

The Return | Melissa Ferrer

The first nine months
Of our life
Was spent
In quarantine
Nurtured by the wisdom
Of our mother's mothers
Nutrified by the Earth
Suckling
As one being in body
Organic
In nature.
Symbiotic
Symbol of continuation.

Why
Have we not returned
Awareness to the womb
In these times
Seek the divine dark
From which the spark of life
Was bourne?

Why
Have we not sought
The wisdom of those who came
Before separation
Before degradation
And desecration of mind
And spirit?

Why
Have we not embraced
The girth of the earth
Beneath our feet?
Learn of what this bigness
Be. Hear what the bees
Buzz; news
Of the Ancient Ascent
And the absence
Of each.

Noise.
Uttered in tongue
And misidentified meaning
Ideological demons
Occupying the homes
Turned house—
The bodies
Turned louse—
Parasitic
Prophet of death
And termination
Living in the fauna
Of our mouths.

Hands balled into fists
Tightness taught us
To savor our anger
As a way to resist
The falling dominoes
And kingdoms
Devoid of glory and
fortified, sanctified

Foundation
Tumbling-- remains
Creating another story—
Debris, and crumbs
Of those numbed
Translated as the way
To salvation.
And thus, the birth of this new nation.

Always and always
More and more
Preaching the gospel of lonely
And fragmentation
Disintegration of awareness
Assimilation of fear
Abandonment of what is
In search of what was never there—
Perfection in the flesh
Salvation in what we can hold
What we can mold
From our dastardly desires—
      A kingdom foretold
      Whose fall approaches.

In the wombs of our rooms
Let us croon ourselves into
Gestation
Into carry
Into hold
Let us sing, sing, sing
Lullabies of light light light
And drift,   drift,   drift
into the silence of the Darkness

That brought us to be

Behind every word that we speak
Let us abandon every pit-
                        ting against

Form us into I
Into one
Into *yo soy*
Io sono
Je suis

Daughter and Son
Husband and Wife
Mother and Father
Sister and Brother
man/woman
Divinity made flesh
Masculine-Feminine
Oneness in our chest
And from this cavity
                      —this hollow—
That breathes
Blood and remembrance
Let us grow our seeds.

Traditio, Patron Saint of Legacy | Paulie Lipman

What will we
leave behind if our
tomorrow is canceled?

No matter
how careful
our remains
they will be
misinterpreted
by whatever is
to follow

All our stories
lost/twisted by
our once proud
voices, now silent
and a new mythos
will emerge

A fable imparts
no knowledge
without context
while a legend's
only education is
in vanity's broken
equation

Distance plus
Time, forsaken
of Moral equals
a hollow monument
and anything built

upon it will surely

fall

The best gift
one could endow
the future is a
solid foundation
set in Compassion
built up into spires
molded in Reason that
will forever provide
a roof, a shelter
walls lined with
books and art
and music

and film that
can never be
leveled
burned
bombed or
blown down by
the seething wind
of Ignorance

Let our legacy
be the only house
left standing in
the wasteland
welcoming all

to not only
take refuge
but learn how
to build their own

AUTHOR BIOS

Cortney Collins is a poet living in Longmont, CO. A four-time winner of Fort Collins' First Friday Poetry Slam at The Bean Cycle, her work has been published by South Broadway Ghost Society, Amethyst Review, Devil's Party Press, Back Patio Press, 24hr Neon Mag, The Naropa Vagina Monologues Zine, and is forthcoming in Tiny Spoon Lit Mag. During these strange and surreal times, she hosts a weekly poetry virtual open mic, Zoem. She shares a home with her beloved cat, Pablo, and tries to eat just the right amount of kale.

Brett Randell is a writer and musician who loves to play in regular venues, on rooftops, at yoga festivals, in bars, living rooms, and beyond. He is currently working on a novel while part of The Book Project at The Lighthouse Writer's Workshop. Brett's writing has appeared in Stain'd Magazine, Interkors, and The Blue Lake Review.

Chelsea Cook grew up on the coast of Virginia, but now calls the mountains of Colorado home. She has been writing poetry since high school, and has been active in the Boulder open mic scene. She is currently finishing the draft of her first novel.

Patricia McCrystal is a fiction writer and poet from Denver, Colorado. She is the recent recipient of the Slippery Elm 2020 Prose Prize. She's currently pursuing her MFA in Fiction at Regis University, and is the founder of VIRAGO, a Denver-based womxn's creative writing circle. Her work can be found on the stage on PBS, and on the page in Heavy Feather Review, South Broadway Ghost Society, Fellow Magazine, Birdy Magazine, and more.

Bruce Sterling Who is this Sterling character? Some call him philosopher, some call him dad. Nobody calls him a poet but that doesn't stop him from crafting lines into something just about good enough to read. Without any formal training he seems to hold his own at the beloved Writer's Block's weekly writing events. He's known to say, "Spending time with the poetry community is the only sane thing to do in this world. It fosters creativity, acceptance and huge amounts of love and frankly not much else matters." Bruce is published in Spit Poet and Writer's Block zines.

Mallary McHenry Jr. (Poet Without Apology) and **Jovan Mays** were members of Denver's Slam Nuba, a nationally ranked poetry slam team. Both have a mutual passion for poetry and helping those in need. "My Mother's Recipe" is a poem dedicated to Mrs. McHenry and all the women who grew up feeling the weight of Jim Crow. Their life experiences cooked into every meal and their recipes cannot be duplicated without understanding the struggles that made them.

Maria S. Picone has an MFA from Goddard College. She's interested in cultural issues, identity, and memory. As a Korean adoptee in an Italian American family and a New Englander, her obsessions with noodles, seafood, and the ocean are hardly her fault. Her poetry appears in Homestead Review, Ariel Chart, Headline Poetry, Mineral Lit Mag, and Route 7 Review. Her Twitter is @mspicone, and her website is mariaspicone.com.

Nate Ragolia is Co-Founder of Spaceboy Books LLC., a Denver-based indie sci-fi press. He's also Editor-in-Chief of BONED: A Collection of Skeletal Writings. His two books, There You Feel Free and The Retroactivist express his ongoing frustrations with economic systems designed to leave people behind. And he's hopeful that things can still be changed for the better in his lifetime.

Caleb Ferganchick is a queer slam poet residing in Grand Junction, CO. He is the self-published author of "Poetry Heels." His work gravitates toward gender and sexuality expression, LGBTQI+ liberation, trauma, and mental health, though he is currently exploring nature writing inspired by rural Western Colorado through a children's book series. Ferganchick hosts an annual poetry slam competition in Grand Junction, "Slamming Bricks," during Colorado West Pride's Festival in honor of the 1969 Stonewall Riots. When he is not writing, Ferganchick works for a non-profit organization dedicated to ending youth homelessness, and as a high school speech and debate coach.

Dennis Etzel Jr. lives in Topeka, Kansas with Carrie and the boys where he teaches English at Washburn University. His work has appeared in *Denver Quarterly, Indiana Review, BlazeVOX, Fact-Simile, 1913: a journal of poetic forms, 3:AM, Tarpaulin Sky, DIAGRAM,* and others.

Ted Vaca, is a Denver poet and spearheaded the origin of The Mercury Cafe Poetry Slam in 1998. He is a member of the Championship Slam team from Asheville NC winning in Ann Arbor MI in '95 and the couch of the Championship team from Denver winning in Austin TX in 2006. His work has been published in a hand full of small publications. He currently resides in Lakewood, CO where he lives with his partner Lisa, their son and 2 cats.

Stina French writes mystery, magic-realism, flash memoir, and poetry. She's featured in many Colorado venues, and her work has appeared in *Heavy Feather Review, Punch Drunk Press,* and the podcast *Witchcraftsy.* She is scratching at the window of her body, writing poems like passwords to get back in. To get forgiven. To get at something like the truth. To get it to go down easy, or at all. She wears welts from the Bible Belt, her mother's eyes in the red fall. She's gone, hypergraphic. Writes on mirrors, car windows, shower walls. Buy her a drink or an expo marker.

Iris Groot (they/them) They call me many things, a beautiful disaster, a cartoon flower, a poem. But most of the time they call me Iris. I'm a non-binary babe who sprinkles poetry around Colorado. I'm also a trigger warning to remind you things aren't always as cheery as my smile. You can follow me on instagram cute_little_queer and join my facebook page poetry people. A private group where it's a safe place to share poems with one another.

Liza Sparks (she/her/hers) is a brown, multiracial, pansexual woman living and writing in Colorado. Liza holds her BA in Poetry from Colorado College after attending on an El Pomar Scholarship for leadership and civic engagement. Liza was a finalist for Denver Lighthouse Writer's Workshop Emerging Writer Fellowship in Poetry in 2020 and 2019; and was a semifinalist for Button Poetry's Chapbook Contest in 2018. She has been published with Cosmonauts Avenue, Dirt Media, Tiny Spoon, Suspect Press, and Stain'd Arts. For more of Liza's work, visit www.lizasparks.com or via Instagram @sparksliza534.

Sophie Cardin is a second-year student studying political philosophy and nonviolent theory at Colorado College in Colorado Springs. She was born and raised in Denver. Sophie fell in love with poetry during her early struggles with dyslexia. She is a regular at the Friday Night Poetry Open Mic at the Mercury Cafe and the author of *Lust Poems For No One In Particular.*

Shelsea Ochoa is a creative powerhouse and community activist. She is an improviser, clown, actor, storyteller, howler, teacher, facilitator, and event producer. Sometimes you can find her on Mars teaching kids about space. Other times she is a sheriff solving a murder mystery. More often than not she is cooking surprisingly good meals with ingredients that can be best described as "questionable". (Written by her friend and biggest fan Danny.)

Kevin Quinn Marchman is an actor, producer, teaching artist and writer. He is Co-founder and current Director of Education with the Black Actors Guild. He misses the Denver Nuggets very much and hopes they miss him too.

Charles Dalton Telschow is a 26 year old Colorado native who is set to release his third self-published book of poetry, "a constellation of sparks". He has been performing poetry for over ten years and also has been in the local music scene for almost as long. He has a solo music project called "The Polite Heretic"

Ashley Howell Bunn is pursuing her MFA in poetry through Regis University where she is also a graduate writing consultant. She reads and helps develop community engagement for the literary journal Inverted Syntax. Her work has previously appeared in *The Colorado Sun*, the series *Head Room Sessions*, and others. When she isn't writing, she teaches and practices yoga and runs a small personal business centered around healing. She lives in Denver, CO with her partner and child.

Amy Wray Irish grew up immersed in Chicago's diverse arts scene, then traded Midwest winters for the Rocky Mountains. She has been published both online and in print journals, most recently with *Punch Drunk Press* and *Waving Hands* (forthcoming). Irish is a member of *Lighthouse Writers*, *Columbine Poets*, and *Turkey Buzzard Press*; her chapbooks include *Creation Stories* (2016) and *The Nature of the Mother* (2019).

Jessica Rigney is a poet, artist, and filmmaker. She is *poetjess* on Instagram.

Christopher Woods is a writer and photographer who lives in Chappell Hill, Texas. His photographs can be seen in his gallery - http://christopherwoods.zenfolio.com/ . His photography prompt book for writers, *FROM VISION TO TEXT*, is forthcoming from *PROPERTIUS PRESS*. His novella, *HEARTS IN THE DARK*, is forthcoming from *RUNNING WILD PRESS*.

Varinia Rodriguez once wrote a book about how Jellyfish Dreams were responsible for her own saving. She is raw, intense, and lovely like a shot of whiskey on a cold day hitting like a cup of hot cocoa. She is an alchemist, who works best with fire and the moon. Buy her book of poetry and photography off *Punch Drunk Press*.

Caito Foster is a 26 year old multi-disciplinary artist working predominantly in photography collage and poetry. Caito is the founder and editor of *Spit Poet Publishing* and their flag ship publication and *SpitPoetZine*, started in Denver Colorado in 2018.

Anna Leahy is the author of the nonfiction book *Tumor* and the poetry collections *Aperture* and *Constituents of Matter*. Her work has appeared at *Aeon*, *The Atlantic*, *BuzzFeed*, *The Southern Review*, and elsewhere, and her essays have won top awards from the *Los Angeles Review*, *Ninth Letter*, and *Dogwood*. She directs the MFA in Creative Writing program at Chapman University, where she edits the international *Tab Journal*. See more at www.amleahy.com.

Steve Shultz is a mailman in rural Colorado. Formerly, he was a journalist with *The Denver Post* and *Rocky Mountain News*. His published poetry collections include *Dying While Dreaming, Pancreatic Care Package,* and *FM Ghost*.

Although **Danny Mazur** lives in the shadow of Shelsea's glory, he did form a badass organization called Soul Stories. Check it out, there is nothing else like it. Wiping is something that everyone must learn to do in their coming-of-age story, and we are all here to back Danny up in his journey by using the hashtag #dannymazurlearnstowipe.

David Zaworski Retired just before the pandemic shutdowns, I am sheltering in place with my love in Portland, Oregon. Inspired by Kim Stafford's generous teaching of his father William Stafford's daily writing practice, for several years now I have tried to write every day. Last night I slept in the hammock under the redwood in the backyard.

Roseanna Frechette is a longtime member of Denver's thriving bohemian underground. Spoken word performer and host as well as multi-genre writer, her work has featured at art galleries, rock stages, and festivals including *Poetry Rodeo*, *Boulder Fringe*, and *Arise* as well as indie publications including *Stain'd*, *Lummox*, *Semicolon*, and *Suspect Press*. Former publisher of *Rosebud Forum* magazine, and one of *Westword*'s Colorado Creatives, Roseanna holds great passion for the power of small press and the beauty of literary originality.

Jericho Hockett's roots are in the farm in Kansas, and she is blooming in Topeka with Eddy and Evelynn. She earned her Ph.D. in Social Psychology at Kansas State University, but is a forever student. She is also a poet, teacher, and especially a seeker who is most whole in the green--whether in garden, field, forest, or heart. Her poems appear in *Burning House Press, Snakeroot: A Midwest Resistance 'Zine, Ichabods Speak Out: Poems in the Age of Me, Too, SageWoman, Heartland! Poetry of Love, Resistance, and Solidarity,* and *Touchstone*, with more works always brewing.

Irina Bogomolova is a Russian-born, Colorado local-enough poet who resides in Denver. Irina represented Denver on the 2018 Mercury Café team at the National Poetry Slam in Chicago. In 2019, she was featured on *PBS's Head Room Sessions*. Also in 2019, Irina published her first book titled, *They Will Not Bleed for Us*. In this work Irina explores family, love, society, and art. She also has a CD, a chapbook -*TEASE*, and a broccoli sticker. Outside of her dark poetry, Irina is a damn good time. And really good at writing personal bios and not being awkward about it; while being totally awkward about it. IG: REROUTEPOETRY

Daniel G. Snethen grew up in rural SD on a farm & ranch. He is a teacher on the Pine Ridge Reservation, a naturalist and a poet. Snethen has published numerous poems in both online and print journals. Snethen's favorite poets include Anne Sexton, Marianne More, Lola Ridge and James C. Van Oort. He owns several pets including his two loyal dogs, Knightly & Lucy, two ferrets, a bearded dragon, a prairie rattlesnake named Witten and several other creatures. During the summers he spends his time researching the Federally endangered American burying beetle.

Bill Gainer is a storyteller, humorist, poet, and a maker of mysterious things. He earned his BA from St. Mary's College and his MPA from the University of San Francisco. He is the publisher of the PEN Award winning *R. L. Crow Publications* and is the ongoing host of *Red Alice's Poetry Emporium* (Grass Valley, CA). Gainer is internationally published in such journals and magazines as: *Poems for All, The Huffington Post, Sacramento News and Review, The Tule Review, Lummox Press, River Dog Zine #1, The Oregonian Newspaper, Chiron Review, Sacramento Bee, Cultural Weekly, Rose of Sharon*, and numerous others. His latest book is: "The Mysterious Book of Old Man Poems." Gainer is known across the country for giving fun filled performances. Visit him in his books, at his personal appearances, or at his website: billgainer.com.

Brendan Hamilton is a poet, writer, and history geek who lives in Longmont, CO. He is the author of a collection of poetry, *Jerusalem Plank Road* (Durga Press, 2011). His poems have recently appeared in *EAP: The Magazine* and his nonfiction articles in *Irish in the American Civil War*. He is currently working on a book about reform school boys caught up in the Civil War.

Sarah LaRue is a poet, behavioral health advocate, and activist who loves equally hiding and seeking. Her work has been published in *Staind* and *SoBoGhoSo* publications. Sarah's first book, *i'll just hide until it's perfect*, is available at Mutiny Information Cafe. She is usually found reading all over town, unless she's not.

Guinotte Wise writes and welds steel sculpture on a farm in Resume Speed, Kansas. His short story collection, *Night Train, Cold Beer*, won publication by a university press and enough money to fix the soffits. Five more books since and a five-time Pushcart nominee, his fiction, essays and poetry have been published in numerous literary journals including *Atticus, The MacGuffin, Southern Humanities Review, Rattle* and *The American Journal of Poetry*. His wife has an honest job in the city and drives 100 miles a day to keep it. (Until shelter in place order) Some work is at http://www.wisesculpture.com

Catfish McDaris' most infamous chapbook is *Prying* with Jack Micheline and Charles Bukowski. He's from Albuquerque and Milwaukee. His newest books are *Ghosts of the War Elephants* and *Meat Grinder*.

Matt Clifford is treasurer of Boulder Food Rescue and would just love for you to listen to his band. www.BlackMarketTranslation.rocks www.mattclifford.org

Gwendalynn Roebke is a Black/Brown they/them who likes poems, and on occasion, performs poems.

Leah Mueller is an indie writer and spoken word performer from Bisbee, Arizona. She has published books with numerous small presses. Her most recent volumes, *Misguided Behavior, Tales of Poor Life Choices* (Czykmate Press), *Death and Heartbreak* (Weasel Press), and *Cocktails at Denny's* (Alien Buddha Press) were released in 2019. Leah's work appears in *Blunderbuss, Citron Review, The Spectacle, Miracle Monocle, Outlook Springs, Atticus Review, Your Impossible Voice,* and other publications. She won honorable mention in the 2012 Wergle Flomp Humor Poetry contest.

Liam Max Kelley is a Chilean-American playwright, poet, and 8th grade language arts teacher. He is the program director at *Stain'd Arts,* an arts non-profit based in Denver, Colorado, and the co-founder of *RuddyDuck Theatre Company,* a local absurdist theatre group. He writes poetry to avoid making an argument, to highlight life's horrid ambiguities, and to turn the heads of those around him. (Alas, vanity becomes him.)

Lonnie MF Allen attended the University of Denver for fine arts, but made comics instead. As a result, he cut his teeth for many years in the DIY scene in Denver. A nihilist by day, he transforms into an existentialist from dusk to dawn. As a cartoonist, his artwork and comics have appeared in *The Westword, Birdy, Suspect Press,* and *The Denver Post,* as well as comic publishers *Dark Horse* and *Image Comics*. His comic work has been Eisner nominated, he was named one of Westword's 100 Colorado Creatives, and was the recipient of the prestigious DiNKy Award. Lonnie MF Allen has been the cat-wrangler of the Denver Drink & Draw, a long time cartoonist co-op. He works freelance as a writer, cartoonist, illustrator, and graphic designer.

Jane Ripley is a writer from Illinois and Colorado. She received a BA in Liberal Arts in 1993 from Columbia College, in Chicago. Her chapbook, *Hot Dog Soup* was published in two editions. She has poems in *Punch Drunk Press* online and in *Suspect Press'* Winter edition 2019.

Jennifer Faylor is a Filipino American poet and literary editor whose middle name comes from the Latin for truth. A native of NYC, she now writes verse near the Cascade mountains. She has a choose-your-own-adventure poetry chapbook, *The Case of the Missing Lover* (Dancing Girl Press) and a full-length collection, *Edison's Ghost Machine* (Aldrich Press). She is currently working on a collection of poetry, *Love Letters from Inanimate Objects* with Colorado poet Eric Raanan Fischman.

Jonathan Bluebird Montgomery first wrote this piece six years ago during the more lost time in his life. He dug it out recently (thinking about supermarkets in light of coronavirus) and rewrote it reflecting on how he's changed. It might sound like he's in recovery or something, but really he's just trying to grow up a little. Go to <u>jonathanbluebirdmontgomery.com</u> for more on him and his work.

Shawn Pavey is the author of *Talking to Shadows* (Main Street Rag Press, 2008), *Nobody Steals the Towels From a Motel 6* (Spartan Press, 2015), and *Survival Tips for the Pending Apocalypse* (2019, Spartan Press). He co-founded *The Main Street Rag Literary Journal* and served as an Associate Editor. A graduate of the University of North Carolina's Creative Writing Program, he likes his Tom Waits loud, his bourbon single-barrel, and his basketball Carolina Blue. His infrequently updated blog is at www.shawnpavey.com.

Rosemerry Wahtola Trommer co-hosts *Emerging Form*, a podcast on creative process. She also co-hosts Telluride's *Talking Gourds Poetry Club* and is co-founder of *Secret Agents of Change*. She teaches poetry for mindfulness retreats, women's retreats, scientists, hospice and more. Her poetry has appeared in *O Magazine*, on *A Prairie Home Companion* and in *Rattle.com*. Her most recent collection, *Hush*, won the Halcyon Prize. She is often found in the kitchen baking with her teenage children. One word mantra: Adjust. https://wordwoman.com/

Michael Sage is a Denver resident. He has worked at the Irish Rover Pub on South Broadway since 2014 and has taught Political Science courses at Community College of Denver since 2016.

Umar Nizar is a poet based in Kerala, India. His poems have been published by *Vayavya, Muse India, Culture Cafe, Journal of the British Library* & in *Ibex Press Year's Best Collection*. He has also been broadcast by *All India Radio*.

Jake Riley is a session guitarist and writer from Denver, and he loves you very, very much.

Scout Noa Halpern, at the thought of introducing themselves as a poet to a Google analyst at a cocktail party, makes light popping sounds with their mouth. They never know what life is going to bring them next, but they keep a lemon squeezer and a cup of sugar nearby just in case. Scout has had numerous moments of pure genius, but was always too stoned to write any of them down. Scout approaches most situations with caution, except those that are entirely outlined with yellow caution tape, towards which Scout charges full speed ahead.

Rebecca Hannigan is an assistant fiction editor for *F(r)iction*. Her work has appeared in The Rumpus, Juked, wigleaf, and elsewhere. She will be joining the MFA program at UNC Wilmington in the fall.

Judyth Hill, poet, editor, teacher, is the author of nine books of poetry and the internationally acclaimed poem, *Wage Peace,* published worldwide; set to music, performed and recorded by national choirs and orchestras. She is the current President of PEN San Miguel. Hill conducts poetry and memoir workshops and classes at elementary and high schools and conferences world-round, edits memoirs, novels and poetry manuscripts, and leads global *WildWriting Culinary Adventures* in France, Mexico, Slovenia and Italy. She was described by the St. Helena Examiner as, "Energy with skin" and by the Denver Post as, "A tigress with a pen".

Marcy Rae Henry is a Latina born and raised in Mexican-America/The Borderlands. She was a bit of a hermit before the virus, truth be told. Before all that, she lived in Spain, India and Nepal and once rode a motorcycle through the Middle East. Her fiction and nonfiction have received a Chicago Community Arts Assistance Grant and an Illinois Arts Council Fellowship. Ms. M.R. Henry is working on a collection of poems and two novellas. She is an Associate Professor of Humanities and Fine Arts at Harold Washington College Chicago and a digital minimalist with no social media accounts.

Arlis Mongold: In the day, Arlis markets things. In the night, he writes and paints. He's currently working on a book containing 100 pieces of flash fiction, each 100 words in length.

Sarah Jane Justice is a South Australian creative whose work has been commended in a number of fields. She competed as a national finalist in the *2018 Australian Poetry Slam,* counts four releases of original music to her name, and has seen her poetry and prose published around the world, including in releases from *The Blue Nib, Black Hare Press,* and *Pure Slush*.

Eli Whittington is a poet, parent, tiler, gardener, singer/songwriter and hiker living in Denver, CO. They've been published in *Stain'd Arts Magazine, Punch Drunk Press Anthology, Spit Poet Zine, Black Market Translation's Punketry album,* and multiple times in *Suspect Press'* quarterly arts magazine. Their first collection of poetry, *Treat Me Like You Treat the Earth,* was published by Suspect Press in 2019 and is available in local bookstores and on Suspect Press' website. They've hosted and been featured and DIY art spaces from the Midwest to the West Coast, and continue to dig into what it means to be an artist, builder and dreamer in the times we live in.

s. Nicholas lives and teaches in the mountains above San Bernardino Ca. She has a BA in English/World Literature & Psychology from Pitzer College and an M.F.A. from Cal State San Bernardino. She is currently writing a collection of short stories to which she cannot devise endings.

Gerard Sarnat MD's won the Poetry in Arts First Place Award/Dorfman Prizes; has been nominated for a handful of recent Pushcarts/Best of Net Awards; authored *HOMELESS CHRONICLES* (2010), *Disputes, 17s, Melting The Ice King* (2016). He's widely published including recently by academic-related journals *Stanford, Oberlin, Wesleyan;* as well as *LA Review, San Francisco Magazine, New York Times. Mount Analogue* selected *KADDISH* for distribution nationwide Inauguration Day. Poetry was chosen for a 50th Harvard reunion Dylan symposium. www.gerardsarnat.co

Alexis Rhone Fancher is published in *Best American Poetry, Rattle, Hobart, Verse Daily, Plume, Cleaver, Diode, Poetry East, Flock, Duende, Nashville Review, Pedestal Magazine* and elsewhere. She's authored five poetry collections, most recently, *Junkie Wife (Moon Tide Press, 2018), and The Dead Kid Poems (KYSO Flash Press, 2019).* Her sixth collection, *EROTIC: New & Selected*, publishes in August 2020 from *New York Quarterly,* and another full-length collection (in Italian) will be published in 2021 by *Edizioni Ensemble, Italia.* Her photographs are featured worldwide. A multiple Pushcart Prize and Best of the Net nominee, Alexis is poetry editor of Cultural Weekly. www.alexisrhonefancher.com

Taylor Jones is a conservation biologist by training, and spends her days either trying to save the world or escape it via writing and reading. She is an aficionado of the weirdest things in nature, and hopes to one day meet an alien. Her poetry has been published in *Spit Poet Zine* and *South Broadway Ghost Society,* and her short story *"Flower Children"* received an Honorable Mention in the L. Ron Hubbard Writers of the Future contest. She lives in Denver, Colorado, in a house full of plants.

Robert Beveridge (he/him) makes noise (xterminal.bandcamp.com) and writes poetry in Akron, OH. Recent/upcoming appearances in *Red Coyote Review, Deep South Magazine,* and *Aromatica Poetica,* among others.

Jeff Burt lives in Santa Cruz, California, with his wife. He works in mental health. He grew up in Wisconsin, was tempered in Texas and Nebraska, and found a home in California, though landscapes of the Midwest still populate much of his writing. He has work in *Rabid Oak, Clerestory, Williwaw Journal, Tar River Poetry, Eclectica,* and won the 2017 *Cold Mountain Review Narrative Poetry Prize.*

Sherre Vernon is an educator, a poet and a seeker of a mystical grammar. She has written two award-winning chapbooks: *Green Ink Wings,* her postmodern novella, and *The Name is Perilous,* a collection of spiritual poetry. Sherre was a 2019 recipient of the Parent-Writer Fellowship to Martha's Vineyard Institute of Creative Writing and served as the fiction editor for *Fickle Muses* during its final season. Readers have described Sherre's work as heartbreaking, richly layered, lyrical and intelligent. To read more of her work visit: www.sherrevernon.com/publications

Cicada Musselman (aka Kelly Marie Musselman) is a farmer living in an intentional community in upstate New York where she is in charge of celebrations. She was born and raised on the Front Range in Colorado, and was the summer program director of the *Beyond Academia Free Skool Summer Poetry Camp* for two years and co-editor of *Boar Hog Press' Love Shovel Review #6*. Two of her poems are forthcoming in the July issue of *Buddhist Poetry Review* and she has been published in a number of *Love Shovel Reviews*, in *Punch Drunk Press Anthology 2018*, among others.

Rob Geisen is the author of several books of poetry: *Beautiful Graveyards, Paper Thin, The Aftermath*, and others. He co-hosted a weekly poetry/open mic reading at Album's Bistro and The Burnt Toast on the Hill in Boulder for nearly five years and has occasionally written under the pseudonym Get in the car, Helen. He has worked consistently in the human service field as a social worker for the past twenty years.

Lee Frankel-Goldwater is a PhD student, founder of *Little Drops Press* and a proud member of the Colorado poetry community. By day an environmental educator, by night a performer and organizer. Would rather be traveling with you through the cloud forests or countryside sharing stories, then just about anything else.

Liza Katz Duncan is an MFA candidate at Warren Wilson College and a 2017 recipient of an Amy Award from Poets and Writers. Her poems have appeared in *Poetry Northwest, Poet Lore, the Cortland Review*, and elsewhere. She teaches English as a Second Language in New Jersey.

Hannah Skewes is a writer, photographer, and shameless jaywalker based in Denver. She comes from a journalism background and carries that thread throughout her work, writing either observational and or deeply personal pieces. These days she's focused on new media, poetry, narrative storytelling, essay writing, photojournalism, and sexual violence and suicide prevention.

Kierstin Bridger is a Colorado writer and author of *Demimonde (Lithic Press)*, the *2017 Women Writing the West's Willa Award*. She is also author of a full collection, *All Ember (Urban Farmhouse Press)*. Winner of the Mark Fischer Poetry Prize, the 2015 ACC Writer's Studio award, and short-listed for the Manchester Poetry Competition in the UK. She co-hosts Poetry Voice with poet Uche Ogbuji. Find more of her work in *December, Prairie Schooner, Thrush, and Painted Bride Quarterly*. She earned her MFA at Pacific University. Kierstinbridger.com

Tricia Knoll is a Vermont poet whose work appears widely in journals and anthologies. Her collection *How I Learned To Be White* received the 2018 Indie Book Award for Motivational Poetry. For more, visit her website: triciaknoll.com

Eric Raanan Fischman is an escaped New Yorker and runaway post-Orthodox Jew currently residing in Longmont, Colorado. He teaches at the *Beyond Academia Free Skool* in Nederland and has had work in *The Boulder Weekly, Bombay Gin, Infection House, Rabbit Catastrophe,* and the *Punch Drunk Press Anthology.* He is the author of "Mordy Gets Enlightened," published through *The Little Door at Lunamopolis* in 2017.

Caroline Savery is a consultant, facilitator, and educator specializing in regenerative and cooperative systems; and is a witchy weird wild radical experimentalist (and in need of an editor) kind of poet, producer, and performer based in Denver, Colorado. www.carolinesavery.com

Syed Aamir Sharief Qadri is from the Indian State of J&K (now Union territory). He has completed post-graduation in History from the University of Kashmir. For further studies, he enrolled as a research scholar at Punjabi University, Patiala and completed his M.Phil. there. Currently, he is working as a freelancer and writes for different newspapers as a Guest writer. Besides, he write poems both in English as well as Urdu languages. As a voice of Kashmir, he is specialized in writing poetry against atrocities committed by occupational forces in Kashmir. #Resistancepoetry #Kashmir Issue

mayryanna is a wild spirit that craves freedom and getting wanderlost in nature. They have written songs since they were a young child but didn't recognize the value of their lyrical heart until learning and then unlearning all about poetry as an adult. Eclectic, subversive and sensual, they seek to create art that is inspired by the delightful imperfections of their humanity. Their work is raw and unfixed, flowing from loosed emotional blocks, deep spiritual ties and their curious explorations of the mysterious withinness that animates their life. Discover more of mayryanna's enchantments online at: www.optimalmastery.life.

Mary Christine Delea is a native New Yorker (from Long Island) now living in Oregon. She is a former college professor. Her poems have appeared in over 200 publications, including 1 full-length book and 3 chapbooks. You can find more of her work in recently and upcoming editions of *Moon City Review, The Hollins Critic, Red Earth Review,* and *Garfield Lake Review,* as well as on her web site (mchristinedelea.com).

Grace Mitchell is a poet residing in Denver, CO. She has edited for *Negative Capability Press* and the *Oracle Fine Arts Review,* and her work has been featured previously in *South Broadway Ghost Society.* She enjoys cats and floral prints, and is learning to laugh at her own mistakes.

Steven Sassmann draws a distinction between Poetry and Poems. He writes unintentionally, which is to say that he doesn't begin until he has no choice. He favors Wit and Brevity over Style and Form. His unique Visual Design evolved during the last several years when Facebook was his only venue. This Design and his Content have propelled his Poetry into the top tenth of one percent of the large Poetry groups where he posts. His style developed to compete in today's overly-saturated market for the time and thought of non-Academic readers. Steven will publish his 10th book in 2020. He lives in Smith Center, Kansas with his wife, Mary.

John Staughton is a writer, editor, photographer and publisher with old roots in Chicago, fresh ones in Denver, and a decade of adventures in between. His prose, poetry and photography exorcises struggles of aloneness, from the sacred joys of empty space to the devastating moments of mental isolation.

Veronica Love is a writer of fiction, poetry and editorials. Her work has appeared in several literary journals including *Page and Spine* and *Flash Fiction Addiction*. She spends her free time traveling to places rich with culture, reading, writing and laughing. She is always on the lookout for a new and strange adventure and loves dancing in the rain.

Agnes Vojta grew up in Germany and started writing poetry as a child. She spent a few years in California, Oregon, and England, and now lives in Rolla, Missouri where she teaches physics at Missouri S&T and hikes the Ozarks. She is the author of *Porous Land (Spartan Press, 2019)* and *The Eden of Perhaps (Spartan Press, 2020)*, and her poems have appeared in a variety of magazines.

Connor Orrico is a student and amateur field recordist interested in global health, mental health, and how we make meaning from the stories we share with each other, themes which were recently explored in his publications in *Headline Poetry & Press* and *Plum Tree Tavern*.

Kristin LaFollette is a writer, artist, and photographer, and the author of the chapbook *Body Parts* (GFT Press, 2018). She is a professor at the University of Southern Indiana and serves as the Art Editor at *Mud Season Review*. You can visit her on Twitter at @k_lafollette03 or on her website at kristinlafollette.com.

Nicole Taylor lives in Eugene, Oregon. She has been an artist, a hiker, a poetry note taker, a sketcher, a volunteer and a dancer. Her poems have been accepted in *BareBack Journal - an online Canadian journal; Boneshaker: A Bicycling Almanac; Camel Saloon; Cirque Journal; Just Another Art Movement Journal - New Zealand; West Wind Review* and others. You can read more of her at www.oregonpoeticvoices.org/poet/312 , a collection of Oregon poets with written and audio poetry available online through Lewis & Clark College in Portland, Oregon.

Maggie Saunders is a professional learner. She does her work playfully, as a preschool teacher and poet. She teaches in Boulder, Colorado at a nature and play based child development center. She is inspired by the muse to be found in each moment, and writes in an attempt to capture the multidimensional realities which create them. When she is not playing with written words, she is grateful to spend her days discovering with her preschool students how to be a more compassionate and curious human. Her poems are digitally archived on medium.com/@akashicrecordpoetry.

Wendy Mannis Scher, a graduate of the Low Residency MFA program for Creative Writing/Poetry at the University of Alaska/Anchorage, lives with her family in Colorado's Front Range. Her recent publications include the chapbook, *Fault (Finishing Line Press)*. For additional information, please visit www.wendymscher.com.

Ken Farrell's work has been anthologized/appeared in *Pilgrimage, Sport Literate, Watershed Review, Coffin Bell Journal, The Piltdown Review,* and elsewhere. He holds an MFA from Texas State University and an MA from Salisbury University, and has earned wages as an adjunct, cage fighter, pizzaiolo, and warehouseman. He is currently revising and shopping poetry and fiction, and responding to his daughter's challenge: participated in NaNoWriMo and recently beginning his first novel.

Janette Schafer is a freelance writer, nature photographer, part-time rock singer, and full-time banker living in Pittsburgh, Pennsylvania. Her writing and photographs have appeared in numerous publications. She holds an MFA in Writing from Chatham University. She has a forthcoming chapbook from Main Street Rag Publishing titled *Something Here Will Grow*. For information regarding her work, feel free to email her at Janette.Schafer@gmail.com.

Galen Bernard is the founder of Courage Club, where he helps people make friends with fear. Once a recipient of the Emerging Writer Award from Key West Literary Seminar, he lost his writing voice somewhere in the slush pile while working for Oxford American magazine. Reclaiming wordsmithing as part of his essence has been key in his Colorado life since moving back in 2016. He leads a twice-monthly writing group as a creative playground; search Writing Group Digital Ed. on Facebook to join! You can find more of his work on fear and his stories at @galendares on Instagram or courageclub.co

Anna White grew up in Colorado--first in West Denver off of Evans, then central Denver--before moving to Europe ten years ago to raise her three children. She studied philosophy at college, but now also loves anything and everything that goes by the name of poetry.

Deborah Edler Brown is an award-winning poet, writer, journalist, and author. Her work has appeared in such publications as *Nimrod, So Luminous the Wildflowers, poeticdiversity, Altered Lanes, Blue Arc West,* and *Sisters Singing: Blessings, Prayers, Art, Songs, Poetry & Sacred Stories by Women*. Her poem "Cubism" won Kalliope's Sue Saniel Elkind Poetry Prize, and her fiction has been twice nominated for the Pushcart Prize. Deborah was born in Brazil, raised in Pittsburgh, and earned her degree in Creative Writing from Brown University. She resides in Los Angeles, where she is busy building communities among her characters and readers.

Morgan L. Ventura is a writer, poet, and folklorist living between Oaxaca, Mexico and the Midwest. Ventura's work has appeared or is forthcoming in *Phantom Drift, Ghost City Review,* and *South Broadway Ghost Society,* while their essays have been featured in *Jadaliyya* and *Folklore Thursday*.

Riley Welch is a poet from Texas living in Denver, she is often cold. Her work has appeared in *The Write Launch* and *Authentic Texas Magazine,* among others. She writes about aliens, fake relationships, monsters, and herself. She makes a great loaf of banana bread.

David-Matthew Barnes is an author, playwright, poet, and screenwriter. He writes in multiple genres, primarily young adult. He earned an MFA in Creative Writing at Queens University of Charlotte in North Carolina. He lives in Denver.

Mary Anna Kruch is a career educator and writer, having taught middle and university students over the past 45 years. Presently, she supervises student teachers for Northern Michigan University and leads a monthly writing group. Her poetry is inspired by Mary Anna's Italian family near Rome, long-term relationships, social justice issues, and nature. Some of her recent poetry has appeared in *Wayne Literary Review, Trinity Review, Ariel Chart, The Remembered Arts Journal,* and others, along with three anthologies. Her first poetry collection, *We Draw Breath from the Same Sky,* was published last summer through Finishing Line Press.

Jacob Ian DeCoursey: Between working long hours for little pay, Jacob Ian DeCoursey has contributed articles to *Brutal Planet Magazine* and *Shockwave Magazine,* while his literary credits include *9Tales Told in the Dark, Grub Street, The Welter, Poems from the Heron Clan, The Scum Gentry Alternative Arts & Media, Horror Sleaze Trash,* and *Not One of Us*—among others. In 2019, during a stint of unemployment, he published his first book, *Vivid Greene: and Other Unusual Stories*. He resides in Baltimore, Maryland.

Hayden Dansky is a transgender nonbinary rural queer kid trying their best to not to be smothered by capitalism. They have been writing and performing poetry for several years, and are currently collaborating with local experimental musicians and dancers to create performances that encompass multiple disciplines. They have no published works, but one time a British literary scholar compared them to Shakespeare. They are also the Executive Director of Boulder Food Rescue, a nonprofit working to create a more just and less wasteful food system, through the sustainable redistribution of healthy food and participatory and community-led food access systems.

Melissa Ferrer is a renegade with hippie tendencies. Through poetry she seeks to provide a sense of solidarity to all people, encourage people to act unto peace and love, and foster community among both the like and unlike minded. Recently, she's been yearning to set down her ego and replace it with a jubilation of the spirit. She wants you to join in, in whatever capacity you can.

Paulie Lipman is a former bartender/ bouncer/ record store employee/ Renaissance Fair worker/ two-time National Poetry Slam finalist and a current loud Jewish/ Queer/ poet/ writer/ performer. His work has appeared in *Button Poetry, Write About Now, The Emerson Review, Drunk In A Midnight Choir, Voicemail Poems, pressure gauge, Protimluv (Czech Republic)* and *Prisma: Zeitblatt Fur Text & Sprache (Germany)*. Their poetry collections *from below/denied the light* and *sad bastard soundtrack* are available from Swimming With Elephants Publications

EDITOR BIOS

Emylee Frank is the Social Media Specialist for South Broadway Ghost Society. She helps the Denver band, Saeva, write poems to the sky. Emylee also runs her own Astrology/Mystic theme Instagram, @eclipselunairee. The page is currently on hiatus while she works on improving its content. In the meantime, she has taken on the role as an Editor for Thought For Food and hopes to have the opportunity to edit and collaborate with future anthologies for South Broadway Ghost Society.

Kali Heals is a socially conscious editor, author, multi-genre artist and speaker dedicated to supporting progressive causes and creative community building. They work in non-traditional somatic and talk therapies for individuals, couples, groups and businesses to progress and build from conflict. More information about their method and book on *Communitive Justice* will be available soon. Their dance, acro, spoken word, music project *Midnight Medicine* can be found online. @kaliheals @themidnightmedicine

Erica Hoffmeister is originally from Southern California, but now lives in Denver where she teaches college writing and media literacy. She is the author of two poetry collections: Lived in Bars (Stubborn Mule Press, 2019), and the prize-winning chapbook, Roots Grew Wild (Kingdoms in the Wild Press, 2019), but considers herself a cross-genre writer. She has had a variety of short fiction, creative nonfiction, poetry and articles published in various journals and magazines such as *Drunk Monkeys, Motherly, Suspect Press, Crab Fat Magazine, Bright Wall/Dark Room,* and *Flash Fiction Magazine.* You can learn more about her at: http://www.ericahoffmeister.com/

Brice Maiurro is the Editor-in-Chief of South Broadway Press. He is the Poetry Editor for Suspect Press and the Founding Editor of Punch Drunk Press. He has published two collections of poetry, *Hero Victim Villain* and *Stupid Flowers.* You can find more about him at www.maiurro.co.

THANK YOU

There are so many people to thank for this collection.
Please find our ever-growing list at
www.soboghoso.org/tffthankyou